JB JOSSEY-BASS™
A Wiley Brand

T0342495

How to Get a Planned Gifts Program Up and Running

SECOND EDITION

Scott C. Stevenson, Editor

WILEY

978-1-118-69167-0   ISBN

978-1-118-70422-6   ISBN (online)

How to Get a Planned Gifts Program Up and Running

2nd Edition

Published by

Stevenson, Inc.

P.O. Box 4528 • Sioux City, Iowa • 51104

Phone 712.239.3010 • Fax 712.239.2166

www.stevensoninc.com

TABLE OF CONTENTS

TABLE OF CONTENTS

TABLE OF CONTENTS

How to Get a Planned Gifts Program Up and Running

GETTING STARTED: PLANNING, SETTING GOALS

No nonprofit should be without a planned gifts program regardless of its size or history of charitable gifts. In fact, a solid planned gifts program will actually strengthen annual giving. Remember a planned gifts program represents a long-term investment. Large gifts won't be realized overnight, but when they do begin to materialize, the time and resources invested will be worth it. If you're just getting a planned gifts program started, be sure to engage your board in the process. Seek their input and help them gain ownership of your program. And by all means, be sure to set goals for your program.

Your planned giving effort should begin with a business plan which presents your goals and objectives, the proposed organizational structure, staffing needs, a budget and a timetable that addresses what you intend to accomplish by when.

Convince Board Members to Make Planned Gifts

It's worth your investment of time to convince board members to make planned gifts to your organization.

"Why?" you ask. Several reasons: 1) If board members aren't "sold" on the value of planned gifts to your organization, how can they expect others to make such gifts? 2) Likewise, board members who have made planned gift provisions will be much better equipped to sell others on the idea. 3) Board members — more than any other constituency — should realize the tremendous good that can be accomplished through the realization of major planned gifts over time.

Here are some strategies you can use to convince your board members to make planned gifts to your organization:

- Enlist the assistance of existing planned gift donors to help "sell" your board.
- Use regular meetings to educate board members on various aspects of planned gifts — types of gifts, ways in which they can be directed, naming opportunities and so forth.
- If you have a planned gifts society, invite board members to help host its events.
- Use board meetings to recognize those having made planned gifts.
- Ask individual board members to help in identifying planned gift prospects.
- List the names of your board on all planned gifts materials — brochures, letterhead, newsletters, etc.
- Get your board to own and endorse your planned gifts policies and procedures.

The more your board members "own" your planned gifts program, the more likely they will become to set an example for others to follow.

From 1998 to 2052, no less than $41 trillion will pass from one generation to the next. That's why every nonprofit organization should be proactive in encouraging planned gifts.

Use History, Demographics to Set Planned Gift Goals

Because of the wide fluctuations that inevitably occur in realized planned gifts from year to year, it can be especially challenging to set goals for what you might hope to achieve in the way of planned gifts. However, once a program has been up and running for five or more years, you should be able to set some quantifiable objectives based on a combination of past history and estimated projections:

1. Depending on how long your planned gift program has been in place, determine your organization's five- or 10-year average for realized planned gifts — in terms of both dollar amounts received and number of planned gifts.

2. Based on planned gift expectancies you are aware of, you can produce an in-house schedule of anticipated gifts based on donors' ages and life expectancy tables.

3. If you're able to determine the approximate ages of those in your database, you can get some sense of the number of 65-and-older constituents at present compared to future numbers of those in that same age group. This will allow you to anticipate the size of your prospect pool at any given time with age being the primary factor.

It's important to set quantifiable planned gift goals that may include but not be limited to:

- *Number of new expectancies.*
- *Number of formal solicitations.*
- *Number of estate planning seminars (and number of attendees).*
- *Number of face-to-face calls.*

GETTING STARTED: PLANNING, SETTING GOALS

Tool Helps Start, Strengthen a Planned Giving Program

Keep the many steps of establishing a planned giving program — securing board committment, recruiting planned giving staff, developing giving policies, etc. — straight with an organizational tool like this template developed by nationally-recognized author and consultant Jerold Panas.

Jerold Panas, of Jerold Panas, Linzy & Partners (Chicago, IL), developed a tool specifically to help organizations start a planned giving program or strengthen an existing one.

Shown below, the tool, Coming of Age —The Twenty-One Factors in Designing a Successful Planned Giving Program, is divided into two sections: activity and action.

Even if you have a planned giving program in place, Panas recommends reviewing the steps listed in the tool to make sure your program incorporates all of them. "It is most helpful if you have a consultant who can go through each step and develop ways to put them into practice," he says.

The action section is used to record when activities are completed. "For example, for the first activity, board approval of a planned giving program, you would put the date the board will be meeting to give approval. Each activity has to be time-bonded in order to be effective. If you don't know you have deadlines to meet or hurdles to jump over, there will be no urgency to getting things done."

Source: Jerold Panas, Jerold Panas, Linzy & Partners, Chicago, IL. Phone (312) 222-1212. E-mail: ideas@panaslinzy.com. Website: www.jeroldpanas.com

Content not available in this edition

GETTING STARTED: PLANNING, SETTING GOALS

In a Down Economy, Develop a System to Secure Planned Gifts

Integrating gift planning into your major giving program is one of the top strategies to successfully weather the current economic storm, says Holly McDonough, director of development and gift planning, Minnesota Medical Foundation (Minneapolis, MN).

A planned gift, McDonough explains, is a creative and flexible way for fundraising organizations to ask donors for major gifts. Gift planning creates a bridge for donors looking for opportunities to support your organization when their cash flow and asset base are diminished. This method of giving can open the door for a deeper donor relationship and a larger gift.

What Is a Planned Gift?

A planned gift is a charitable gift that has a guaranteed value slated for a later date. A donor can give planned gifts via:

- ✓ A bequest in one's will.
- ✓ Naming a charity organization in a retirement plan or an insurance policy.
- ✓ Charitable gift annuities (immediate or deferred) using certificates of deposit or money market accounts.
- ✓ Retained life estate.
- ✓ Outright gifts of excess property.
- ✓ Bargain sales using real estate.
- ✓ Charitable lead trusts.
- ✓ Blended gifts.

How to Promote Planned Gifts:

Promoting gift planning can be as simple as incorporating information about these programs into existing advertising for your organization. Advertising techniques may include:

- ✓ Establishing direct mail or telemarketing programs that allow donors to self-identify as having planned gift assets.
- ✓ Educating your major gift officers. By sharing gift-planning options, says McDonough, a gift officer may move a donor from a transactional gift to a transformational gift, allowing for a larger, more meaningful gift.
- ✓ Developing a relationship with gift planning experts. Many planned gifts carry with them complex legal ramifications. While these legalities should not deter gift officers, the gift officers should be able to call upon gift planning experts or property attorneys to assist with more complicated gifts.

Source: Holly McDonough, Director of Development-Gift Planning, Minnesota Medical Foundation at University of Minnesota, Minneapolis, MN. Phone (612) 625-8758. E-mail: h.mcdonough@mmf.umn.edu

---

Learn to Think Like an Estate Planner

For many gift officers, estate planning is a fundraising option that may seem too foreign, complex or messy to pursue.

Karen Ciegler Hansen, attorney with Felhaber Larson Fenlon & Vogt (Minneapolis, MN), disagrees. She sees estate planning as a unique opportunity in this economic climate that can pay off quite well in the long run.

Hansen offers simple tips for the estate-planning novice:

1. **Listen.** Any good gift officer knows the importance of listening to a donor's hopes for his/her gift. With estate gifts, it is important to also listen to the donor's desires and concerns regarding his/her estate plans.

   Some common concerns are:

   - ❑ **Concern for asset value.** Many estate holders worry their assets will be greatly diminished by the time they pass away. To ensure the estate holder leaves sufficient funds to his/her family, use a math formula in the estate plan. While an estate-planning professional will have to work out the logistics, suggest a percentage gift rather than specific dollar amount, so the gift automatically adjusts with changes in the economy. It is also common practice to treat the receiving nonprofit as an additional child in the family.

   - ❑ **Concern for how their inheritance will be used.** Many estate holders may have complex feelings about their heirs' relationships with money. They may feel that their children will not value the inheritance and will spend it inappropriately. In this case, you can advise donors that they can exemplify their own values to their children by leaving a certain percentage of their assets to charity.

   - ❑ **Concern for their heirs' financial well-being.** On the opposite side of the coin, Hansen explains, many philanthropists have concerns that their children will never be financially self-sufficient, due to economic circumstances, disabilities or other issues. In this case, the donor may be open to the possibility of leaving money for his/her children in a trust during that child's lifetime, and mark the remainder for charity.

2. **Be flexible.** In tenuous economic times, clients want flexibility and fewer strings attached to planned gifts and estate plans. Write flexibility clauses into gift contracts so estate holders feel free to adjust committed gifts at any time. This may also increase your odds of securing a gift.

3. **Collaborate.** Estate planners and other professional advisors can guide you through the estate-planning process while helping you to provide donors with the confidence that they have the information needed to make the best philanthropic choices.

Source: Karen Ciegler Hansen, Attorney, Felhaber Larson Fenlon & Vogt, St. Paul, MN. Phone (651) 312-6043. E-mail: khansen@felhaber.com

GETTING STARTED: PLANNING, SETTING GOALS

Five Tips for Making Planned Giving Work for You

Officials at Lawrence University (Appleton, WI) have spent the last two years revamping planned-giving efforts. Through that process, Associate Vice President of Major and Planned Giving Barbara Stack says she has one rule of thumb when it comes to creating and improving planned giving programs: "Keep it simple. Ninety percent of planned gifts are made through bequests, so focus energy on promoting them."

In promoting bequests, Stack says, keep this top-of-mind: "The most compelling messages for bequest promotion . . . focus on legacy, dreams and ensuring that the donor's values live on through the organizations they care about."

Stack identifies five specific guidelines that Lawrence University officials are using to make their planned giving programs stronger:

1. **Talk to younger donors about retirement assets.** Stack says this allows them to consider your organization earlier in life, which means they are less likely to need convincing later.

2. **Remember that getting started in planned giving doesn't need to be expensive.** "There is so much information, good material, solid advice and quality vendors in our line of work," she says. "Don't get caught up in the fancy tools unless you have trusted advisors who will work with you to do it right (e.g., CGAs, trusts, real estate, etc.)."

3. **Put your donors and your mission front and center.** "This is the best and most effective way to raise funds generally, but especially with planned gifts," says Stack. "Allow your best marketing partners — those who have already 'done it' — to feel great about their decision by allowing them to share their philanthropic journey. Allow the beneficiaries of your mission to express their own thanks to help illustrate what gifts accomplish."

4. **Have a quality web presence** and piggyback your planned giving message with other logical communications from your organization.

5. **Measure your planned giving efforts by tracking meaningful contacts and visits with prospects and donors.** Provide stellar follow up and stewardship, and ensure you have the knowledge and resources to respond to inquiries.

"Most importantly, do not lose sight of why you are doing what you are doing," says Stack. "Planned gifts are not great because of tax advantages or glossy brochures or newsletters. They are another means to an end of fulfilling a donor's wishes to help your organization because it matters to them. If you always focus on the mission and helping donors find ways to support that mission . . . you will be doing your best work for your cause and your donors."

Source: Barbara J. Stack, Associate Vice President of Major and Planned Giving, Lawrence University, Appleton, WI. Phone (920) 832-6546. E-mail: barbara.j.stack@lawrence.edu

Planned Giving Requires Donor-centric Focus

Barbara Stack, associate vice president of major and planned giving at Lawrence University (Appleton, WI), discusses some of the challenges university officials have encountered and changes they have made through a recent two-year renovation of the university's planned-giving efforts:

What sort of unique things are you working on in the area of planned giving?

"We developed a unique peer-outreach approach to our program, giving it a distinct Lawrence 'face.' We have about 35 volunteers who are members of our legacy recognition society who assist us in promoting planned giving to their fellow alumni and constituents who live in their regions across the country. The members help us raise visibility and recruit new members by hosting small parties with prospects, writing notes thanking new members, providing testimonials at events and in printed and electronic materials, serving in leadership roles for planned-gift promotion as they approach milestone reunions and advising us on our website and printed marketing materials."

What have been your biggest challenges in terms of planned giving, and how have you worked to overcome them?

"Our challenges stem from those things we cannot control, like fiscal caution resulting from the recent economic climate. This has provided us with both challenge and opportunity. Over the past couple of years, our donors and prospects have generally been skittish about making any changes to their financial or long-term plans, because they are uncertain about the future. We've addressed those concerns by being patient, continuing to focus on our mission and assuring donors that we work on their timeline and will be here when they're ready. At the same time, our donors have been more receptive to discussing how they might accomplish their philanthropic vision and dreams without jeopardizing their current situation. Due to these conversations, we were able to help our planned gift donors and prospects feel satisfaction by participating in our capital campaign through joining our legacy society and estimating future gifts that could be counted in our campaign."

Focus on Professional Advisors Helpful, Too

The recent planned-giving program revamp at Lawrence University (Appleton, WI) calls for engaging and educating local professional advisors such as wealth and trust managers, estate planning attorneys, tax and insurance professionals who can positively influence and assist their clients with charitable-giving decisions. Barbara Stack, associate vice president of major and planned giving, shares a specific example of how this effort is already making an impact:

"A local attorney who knew that his client had made a provision in his will for Lawrence had become more educated and interested in Lawrence's programs because of our professional advisor outreach. The attorney shared information about the amount required to endow a scholarship, which was a little more than what the client had already planned in his estate, but which is something the client was very excited about doing when it was explained to him.

"The client updated his will, ensuring the estate provision would meet the endowed scholarship. He also shared that news with Lawrence, allowing us to thank him and discuss priorities for his scholarship gift, which were documented for the future. We expect this type of scenario to be the end result of the efforts we are making to form meaningful relationships with these professionals."

GETTING STARTED: PLANNING, SETTING GOALS

Invite Planned Gift Donors to Make Board Testimonials

You'd think that asking members of nonprofit boards to make planned gifts would be like preaching to the choir. But ,in reality, many nonprofit boards don't set the example they should be expected to when it comes to making planned gifts. If this is the case in your nonprofit, you may want to invite a willing planned gift donor to attend a regular board meeting to explain what motivated him/her to make a planned gift.

In addition to motivating board members to make planned gifts, the presentation of a planned gift donor before your board is a wonderful way to recognize him/her and to formally say thank you.

You can be sure that those board members who elect to make a planned gift to your organization will be much more qualified to encourage others to consider establishing planned gifts as well.

Rule of Thumb

■ Expectancies are planned gift commitments known to have been made to your charity but not yet realized (because the donor is still living). As a guide only, you may assume that your charity is aware of one in six such expectancies in advance of receiving them. Example: If you know of 10 expectancies, there are probably at least 60 expectancies to be received at some point.

Secure a Challenge That Leverages Planned Gifts

Have you ever heard of a challenge gift as a way to encourage more planned gifts? Here's how that might work:

Approach a financially capable donor — someone who already recognizes the importance of your planned gift program — to establish a $250,000 outright gift to use as a challenge: Any donor who establishes an irrevocable planned gift of $25,000 or more in the current fiscal year will have $25,000 added to the named fund (by the challenger) he/she sets up.

That would mean that up to 10 individuals who make irrevocable planned gifts would immediately have $25,000 added to an endowment fund in their names. Then, after their lifetimes, their bequests would be added to their funds as well.

No challenge donor willing to step up to the plate? Here's another option: If you already have general endowment dollars not tied to a specific fund and are just part of your general endowment, earmark $25,000 per person to establish the named fund in honor of each planned gift donor.

What a motivator that would be — to have someone match your irrevocable planned gift, so the named fund would begin immediately!

Challenge gifts can sometimes be used to nudge prospects into making a planned gift.

Maximize Time Spent Nurturing Planned Gifts

What can planned gifts officers do to make the most of their time? Here's how several planned gift veterans responded:

Here are some practical ways to make the most of your time.

1. Get to know agents of wealth: attorneys, trust officers, accountants and insurance agents who can help to broaden your efforts.

2. Keep building and fine-tuning your mailing list of prospect names who receive regular information on planned gift issues from your cause.

3. Properly steward existing planned gift donors.

4. Offer various types of estate planning seminars that will put you in touch with likely prospects and enhance your planned gift credentials.

5. Set challenging but realistic planned gift goals for yourself (e.g., number of calls per week, number of new planned gift expectancies per year, number of estate planning seminars).

6. Initiate or build on your planned gifts club or society that recognizes those who have made planned gift provisions.

7. Faithfully publicize bequests and other forms of planned gifts as a way to recognize donors and promote similar gifts.

8. Stay abreast of laws, tax implications and other issues that impact planned gifts and nonprofits.

Justify an Increase To Your Planned Gifts Budget

Whether you're attempting to establish a first-time planned gifts budget or hoping to enlarge it, here are three key criteria for justifying the needed funds:

1. What has been your organization's cost for previously received planned gifts? That cost-to-revenue ratio alone may make your case.

2. Compare your budget to the known amount of collective expectancies.

3. What's budgeted for donors making outright gifts of $10,000 or more?

GETTING STARTED: PLANNING, SETTING GOALS

Get Your Board Engaged In Backing Planned Gifts Programs

Your board's support (or lack of it) for your planned gifts program will impact its long-term success. Enthusiastic support can accelerate planned gifts tremendously.

Consider these steps to strengthen your board's commitment to and involvement in marketing planned gifts:

It's crucial that your board assume ownership of your planned gifts program. Ask them to approve planned giving policies and procedures as a way to engage them in your program.

- Evaluate planned giving programs of nonprofits more advanced than yours and share findings with your board to raise your board's sights.

- Work with your board to establish planned gift goals. Engage members in shaping challenging yet realistic goals.

- Involve your board in establishing and evaluating a planned gifts policy. Does your nonprofit accept charitable remainder unitrusts? Should the board OK accepting bequests that include restrictions? Addressing such ongoing questions establishes the foundation of your planned gifts program and engages board members.

- Set a yearly calendar of activities and events inviting board participation: estate planning seminars, recognition of planned gift donors and more.

- Involve board members in shaping your planned giving budget. Share an itemized budget to show what you are able to accomplish plus what additional resources could do.

- Recognize board members who give time and support to your planned gifts efforts to keep them motivated and also encourage others to become more involved.

- Meet one-on-one with board members to seek their input and expertise. Invite board members to make referrals and help in the cultivation of likely prospects.

- Invite individual board members to make planned gift commitments to your cause.

- Keep board members abreast of information affecting the world of planned giving: issues being addressed at the national level, demographics and more.

Establish Planned Gift Goals

Involve your board in establishing quantifiable objectives that move your program forward in securing new planned gifts. Consider goals such as:

- ❑ To identify ___ planned gift prospects in the current fiscal year.

- ❑ To average ___ personal visits each week with planned gift prospects.

- ❑ To solicit a minimum of ___ planned gifts throughout the current fiscal year.

- ❑ To secure ___ planned gift expectancies amounting to at least $___ during the current fiscal year.

- ❑ To expand the planned gifts mailing list by ___ during the current year.

- ❑ To conduct ___ estate planning seminars during the current year.

- ❑ To enlist ___ centers of influence who will assist our planned gifts efforts by identifying and cultivating would-be donors.

- ❑ To invite all board members to consider our charity in estate plans.

You Needn't Be an Expert To Market Planned Gifts

- ■ Did you know that about 80 percent of all planned gifts come in the form of bequests? That's why, no matter the size of your development shop, you don't need to be an expert to encourage and market planned gifts.

GETTING STARTED: PLANNING, SETTING GOALS

Strategies for Staying Productive While on the Road

As a regional development director at the University of Minnesota Foundation (Minneapolis, MN), Tom Kinsey understands the challenges of fundraising on the road.

"The hardest part is always orienting yourself around the next trip, while simultaneously doing follow-up from the previous two or three trips," Kinsey says. "Being able to juggle those competing demands is what allows people to be successful at this kind of work."

Kinsey shares some tips he has learned over years and miles:

What is the key to being an effective traveling development officer?

"It always goes back to how well organized you are. I once had a boss in sales who said, 'Tom, doing good paperwork will never make you a good salesman, but bad paperwork has ruined many good salesmen.' Tending to mundane details isn't sexy, but it's the foundation of everything else."

Do you have any tips for prioritizing tasks and activities?

"I don't believe that just because e-mail is in your inbox you have to look at it. I will often not check my e-mail until midday, because there are simply too many things that have to get done. Similarly, when I'm on the road I will answer time-sensitive e-mails but try to leave the rest for when I'm back in the office."

How can development officers best use down time on the road?

"I will often take files on alumni living in the area I am visiting and make phone calls between other engagements. Sometimes I can even add an appointment or two to my trip."

Are there fundraising tasks that don't lend themselves to being done on the road?

"I write call notes while on the road but leave full reports for when I am back in the office. Many development officers do them while traveling, but I find that unless the calls are very simple, I don't write as productively or clearly on the road."

Do you have any tips for staying sharp when you have been traveling?

"Consciously focusing on your desired outcomes before entering a call can bring a great deal of clarity. For example, you might say to yourself, 'When I walk through that door I want to bring them greetings, I want them to get to know me a little, and I want to find out if they have any questions about the psych department.'"

How can support staff best be used on the road?

"Prior to the trip, support staff can prepare materials needed for the calls. When actually on the road, I frequently ask for background work on questions that come up during meetings. Often that means contacting department heads, program liaisons and other resource people who can be hard to get ahold of."

Are there limits to how productive you can or should try to be when traveling?

"I gave up working on airplanes years ago. If something is urgent, I'll take care of it on the plane, otherwise I just read a book or sleep. This hasn't appreciably detracted from my productivity, and sometimes just getting a breather from the office is the best thing you can do."

Do you have any practical tips for someone starting a first traveling position?

"If you're checking your baggage, always hand-carry the files you need for the first two days of calls. Your luggage will usually catch up to you by the third day, but you want to be able to work until then."

Source: Tom Kinsey, Regional Development Director, University of Minnesota Foundation, Minneapolis, MN. Phone (612) 624-3333. E-mail: kinse004@umn.edu

Regular personal visits go hand-in-hand with planned giving efforts. Those visits oftentimes include a good deal of road time. Though tiring, business trips can actually be a relatively distraction-free time to catch up on odd jobs and tasks.

GETTING STARTED: PLANNING, SETTING GOALS

Stay Focused on Bequests

Even with the sophistication of some planned gift shops, bequests still account for about 70 percent or more of all planned gift types. That's why you can represent a one-person development operation and still promote planned gifts.

So what are you doing to market bequests to constituents? Here's a checklist of ideas from which to draw:

You need not become an expert in every facet of planned gift options.

- At least once a year, invite everyone on your mailing list to consider making a bequest to your organization.

- Include an article in every newsletter or magazine about some aspect of bequests: sample wording for a will that has a bequest to your organization, a profile of how a realized bequest is impacting your organization and its programs, etc.

- Share anecdotes about bequests made to other nonprofits and how those gifts transformed the organization.

- On all pledge forms, brochures and literature you produce, include the phrase, "Please provide me with additional information about making bequests," along with an address, e-mail or phone number to receive that information.

- Seek the permission of those who have made bequest provisions to publicize their intent among select groups of prospects.

Planned Gift Facts You Should Know

Did you know....

- Estates valued in excess of $1 million will likely include a charitable bequest?

- The likelihood of a charitable bequest is higher among surviving spouses than among the first to die?

- Eighty percent of individuals who contribute annually to charities do not have a will?

How to Get a Planned Gifts Program Up and Running, Second Edition.
Edited by Scott C. Stevenson.
© 2011 Stevenson, Inc. Published 2011 by Stevenson, Inc.

PROSPECT IDENTIFICATION, BUILDING A LIST

Who should make up your planned gifts prospect list? Begin with those who have shown loyalty to your organization. One key measure of loyalty is based on who gives most consistently to your annual fund. For starters, include current and former board members, select current and former employees, those on your mailing list who are age 60 or older, those in your community with no apparent heirs, agents of wealth and others you deem appropriate.

Starting From Scratch? Build a Planned Gifts Prospect List

If you're just getting started with a planned gifts program, a key first step is to build a database of qualified names.

While those persons on your mailing list who have reached retirement make obvious prospects, it's important to screen and rescreen your list. Likewise, age should not prevent someone from being added. After all, life insurance is one of the most affordable major gifts a young person can make.

As you review names to be added to your list, consider:

There are some practical steps you can take to build your list of planned gift prospects.

- Individuals or married couples with no apparent heirs. This characteristic, when combined with senior citizen status, represents obvious candidates for planned gifts.

- Those who have made consistent gifts to your organization over a long period of time, regardless of gift size.

- Persons who have served as volunteers or board members or received awards from your organization in past years.

- Current and former longtime employees.

- Those who support many nonprofits in your community, as this proven level of philanthropy may qualify them as planned gift prospects.

- Agents of wealth: trust officers, attorneys, accountants, insurance agents and other financial planners. While these professionals may not make a planned gift themselves, they can be helpful in influencing others by virtue of association with your organization.

Identify Planned Giving Prospects Among Your Donor Base

Donors who currently give to your organization's annual fund or have made gifts to your capital campaign are great prospects for planned gifts. Your donor database has a wealth of information about current donors. That information is filled with clues about which donors may be great candidates for planned gifts. Here's what to consider:

Prospect identification is an important first step.

- ▶ Women using Miss as a title — a possible indication that they're older and have no heirs.
- ▶ Those whose address indicates they have moved to a retirement community.
- ▶ Donors who have recently given multiple memorial gifts.
- ▶ Donors who have given over a period of 10 years or more, regardless of gift size.
- ▶ Alumni donors whose children or grandchildren also attended your school.
- ▶ Middle-aged (or older) donors who have no children.
- ▶ Those who have served as board members, advisory board members or volunteers.
- ▶ Those exploring gift options for their heirs (children and/or grandchildren). Many planned giving vehicles can help these donors continue to provide for their heirs.

Here's another great way to identify planned giving prospects among your donor base: Profile your existing planned giving donors, looking for similarities in gender, type of planned gift made, age range, number of years giving and geographical location, then search your database for donors who fit those parameters.

PROSPECT IDENTIFICATION, BUILDING A LIST

Work to Identify and Cultivate Children of Wealth

It's common for most nonprofits to focus on those with existing wealth. To lay the groundwork for major gifts that may not materialize for 10 or 20 years, develop a plan aimed at cultivating children of wealth.

Your community is full of individuals in their 30s, 40s and even 50s who are not yet in positions that enable them to make five- or six-figure gifts but will be in 10 or 20 years by virtue of their positions or inherited wealth.

Begin to cultivate those up-and-comers now with a plan that's unique to your organization. Here's one generic scenario that helps illustrate how to do it:

It's never too soon to begin cultivating relationships with children of wealth.

1. Launch some sort of young leaders society that is exclusive to 30- to 50-year-olds who contribute $1,000 or more annually to your organization.

2. Create a steering committee made of those donors who can take ownership in the effort and design a plan catering to the interests of this age group. The steering committee can come up with social activities, member perks, donor recognition ideas, etc.

3. Encourage the committee to establish an annual awards program that recognizes its members in various categories (e.g., professional achievement, philanthropic efforts, volunteer contributions, etc.).

When members turn 51, induct them into a more traditional, inclusive $1,000-and-above gift club. Hold an annual "graduation ceremony" that welcomes them into the older crowd.

The Young Can Establish Planned Gifts, Too

Who says younger persons aren't interested in making planned gifts?

Even if younger constituency members do not receive every planned gift communication produced by your organization, it may be wise to market specific planned gift opportunities to them as well.

Consider the following possibilities:

- **Gift annuities honoring parents.** Why not encourage younger individuals to honor their parents or other older relatives with a named fund? Because the annuity is tied to the age of the older adult(s), the annual rate of return will be higher and more attractive to donors.

- **Life insurance policies.** Life insurance is often referred to as the affordable major gift since a major gift can be established using much smaller gifts equal to annual insurance premiums. (And premiums are lower at a younger age.)

- **Bequests.** Encourage younger donors to include bequests in their estate plans, regardless of amount.

If and when you have younger donors who establish planned gifts, seek their approval to publicize their generosity as one way to encourage other young prospects to follow suit. Publicity can include testimonials, features in your magazine/newsletter, recognition at certain public events and more.

Key Planned Gift Variables

When it comes to identifying the choicest planned gift prospects, the key variables to weigh are not necessarily size of recent gifts or even financial capability. Rather, key variables to consider are:

- What the prospect perceives to be the personal benefits of making a planned gift.

- The prospect's age.

- Consistency in giving over time.

- Connection to your organization.

- Beliefs that are consistent with your non-profit's mission.

PROSPECT IDENTIFICATION, BUILDING A LIST

Estate Gift Predictive Model Increases Efficiency, Allows Age-targeted Marketing

Frank Robertson, director of planned giving at the University of Minnesota Foundation (Minneapolis, MN), can trace the birth of its estate gift predictive model to a single incident:

"A single woman, never married and no heirs, made small annual gifts for decades, but was never identified as a major gift prospect and was never personally contacted. No one knew this woman, but she ended up leaving the university more than $3 million. The potential lost in that relationship was what really prompted us to start looking for a more reliable way of identifying potential estate donors."

The predictive model uses factors common to many estate gift donors, such as consistency of annual giving and marital status, to rate a prospect's likelihood of leaving a gift to the university. The approach allows the foundation to more effectively identify potential donors while extending fundraising efforts to younger demographics without wasting resources, says Robertson.

He shares two examples of how the model has facilitated a focus on younger prospects:

1. **Targeted newsletters.** The foundation maintains two versions of a fundraising newsletter — one targeting donors age 55-64 and one, donors age 65-plus. With the estate gift predictive model, the floor was dropped to age 40 and distribution limited to likely donors. As a result, the foundation mails fewer copies, but reaches more people who are likely to give, at a younger age.

2. **Will survey.** Collegiate units of the university send periodic surveys (see boxed story) seeking confirmation of estate gift commitments to the university. The first year the foundation dropped the minimum age of recipient from 65 to 40 and contacted only the top two designations of the predictive model (very likely and likely to give categories), they posted a 4.1 percent response rate and received seven new estate commitments from donors under age 65.

Source: Frank Robertson, Director of Planned Giving, University of Minnesota Foundation, Minneapolis, MN. Phone (612) 625-0893. E-mail: Rober038@umn.edu

Content not available in this edition

Will Surveys Document Decisions, Plant Ideas

Research shows that once people include a charity in their will they rarely take it out, especially if their gift is properly stewarded, says Frank Robertson, director of planned giving at the University of Minnesota Foundation (Minneapolis, MN). To reach potential donors and foster a culture of planned estate giving, foundation and university staff use a version of the generic will survey, above.

Sent to prospects identified by the foundation's estate gift predictive model, Robertson says the survey documents gift commitments already made, which allows new donors to be incorporated into the stewardship process. It also provides a natural way to introduce potential donors to the idea of establishing an estate gift of their own.

The following results from one survey sent in 2010 attest to the efficacy of the approach:

- Surveys mailed: 5,251
- Surveys returned: 217
- Response rate: 4.1 percent
- New gifts recorded: 19
- Previous gifts reaffirmed: 7
- Gifts from those below the age of 65: 7
- Prospects considering an estate gift and requesting further follow-up: 26

With persons making retirement and estate decisions at increasingly earlier ages, Robertson and his staff recently dropped the survey's age threshold to 40. "We're trying to reach people when they're facing some changes in life and starting to think about the future. The period when they are starting to formulate retirement and estate plans is a great time to begin a conversation about planned giving."

PROSPECT IDENTIFICATION, BUILDING A LIST

Encourage Employees to Make Planned Gifts

Don't overlook loyal employees and former employees as planned gift donors.

Do you know who, among your employees, has no immediate heirs?

Most charities have individuals who are committed employees with no obvious heirs. And even if they do have heirs, they may be open to the idea of making a planned gift. It doesn't matter whether those persons are making large gifts or even smaller annual gifts to your organization. It does matter, however, that you recognize their ability to make a lasting planned gift to the organization they so dearly love.

To help encourage former and current employees to consider making a planned gift:

1. Involve them as volunteers in any capacity in your planned gifts program: helping with heritage society events, writing for your planned gifts newsletter, helping you host an estate planning seminar and more.

2. Begin to explore planned gift opportunities that could positively impact those programs or services that matter most to them as employees.

3. Publicize and/or share examples of planned gifts from your organization — or other charities — that were made possible by employees.

4. Include at least one employee on your planned gifts committee or advisory council.

Turn Current Donors Into Estate Donors and Vice Versa

Get in the habit of making a double ask that addresses both annual and planned giving.

Frank Robertson, director of planned giving at the University of Minnesota Foundation (Minneapolis, MN), says that when it comes to fundraising, "we don't look at individuals as being either only estate donors or only current donors. Ideally, we think they should be both, and we think that, given the right circumstances, many will be."

Accordingly, Robertson and his staff encourage multiple forms of giving. One technique they use is what is known as the double ask. "The idea is that whenever you are asking for a major gift or an annual gift, you also bring up the idea of including the university in your estate plans," he says. "It's a relatively low-pressure approach and many of our development officers have come to really believe in it."

A robust stewardship process is another key to multiplying support, he says. All donors of future gifts, regardless of whether the amount is disclosed, receive membership in the university's Heritage Society. This introduces them to the stewardship process, which is important, according to Robertson.

"If someone is planning on establishing a scholarship upon their death, might they not want to start realizing that good work during their lifetime?" he says. "We find that including estate donors in the stewardship process not only cements their relationship with us and their estate plans, but often leads to other outright gifts."

Source: Frank Robertson, Director of Planned Giving, University of Minnesota Foundation, McNamara Alumni Center, Minneapolis, MN. Phone (612) 625-0893. E-mail: Rober038@umn.edu

INVOLVE VOLUNTEERS, NURTURE A PLANNED GIFTS COMMITTEE

Your ability to build awareness of your planned gifts program will be somewhat dependent on your ability to involve people in identifying would-be donors and cultivating relationships with them. Look for ways to engage volunteers in your planned gifts program, and by all means, establish some sort of planned gifts advisory group whose responsibility is to meet regularly to review policies, identify and nurture planned gift prospects, steward and recognize existing planned gift donors and more.

Engage Volunteers in Planned Gift Development

Whether your planned gifts program is simple or sophisticated, engaging volunteers makes good sense. Anything others can do will multiply your planned gift efforts and increase the probability of receiving more planned gifts. Plus, the very act of involving those individuals will increase the likelihood that they will consider planned gifts as well.

Here are some examples of how to involve volunteers in your planned gifts effort:

❑ **Assemble a planned gifts advisory committee** to review (or create) your planned gifts policies and oversee your program. Include agents of wealth (attorneys, trust officers, accountants, insurance agents), planned gift donors and prospects.

❑ **Enlist small committees in key communities/regions.** Ask participants to serve as ambassadors on your behalf, identifying and cultivating friendships with prospects.

❑ Enlist professionals and friends of your nonprofit to help **conduct an estate planning seminar.**

❑ Ask existing planned gift donors to **write brief articles or offer testimonials** as to why they made the gift. Use in brochures, planned gifts newsletter and at events.

❑ Ask appropriate volunteers or board members to **sign a letter directed to planned gift prospects.**

❑ **Establish a heritage society** coordinated by volunteers to recognize those individuals who have established planned gifts.

Volunteers can help to multiply your planned gift efforts in a variety of ways.

Build an Active, Accomplished Planned Gifts Committee

Many nonprofits take the time to form a planned gifts committee that meets occasionally but accomplishes little. That's a waste of everyone's time.

To build an active planned gifts committee, one whose members are really working to help promote and assist with planned gifts activities:

Make expectations clear. Develop a roles and responsibilities statement that sets forth both group and individual expectations for the members of your committee. Review those responsibilities with committee candidates prior to their appointments.

Assist your committee in setting yearly goals that include quantifiable objectives (e.g., to individually identify and meet with no fewer than 10 planned gift prospects throughout the year).

Schedule regular meetings that include individual assignments. In addition to reviewing and approving planned gift policies, ask your chair to assign specific tasks to members (e.g., contacting prospects, calling on attorneys, participating in a planned gift seminar).

Give them the recognition they deserve. Devote a page to this group on your website, including photos and brief biographies. List their names on planned gift letterhead and in your planned gifts newsletter. Publicly introduce them at estate planning seminars and other related events.

Planned Gift Committees Should Include the Creative

Don't limit your planned gift advisory group to attorneys, trust officers, accountants and insurance representatives. Be sure to include less technical persons who might have creative marketing ideas to offer — public relations or sales specialists, for example.

The addition of nontechnical individuals will help your group look for new and creative ways to market planned gifts and steward those who have already expressed interest in your programs.

INVOLVE VOLUNTEERS, NURTURE A PLANNED GIFTS COMMITTEE

Convince Centers of Influence to Promote Your Cause

Is one of your objectives to promote planned gifts? Then it's in your best interest to convince centers of influence to promote your charity, within ethical limits, to those who use their services.

But before these centers of influence can be convinced to promote your cause, they must first believe in your mission and goals themselves. So how do you compete for their loyalty among a sea of other worthy causes also vying for their attention?

First, you enlist and regularly involve centers of influence in your planned gifts program and help them to visualize what the realization of planned gifts will do to change your organization and benefit those you serve. As they buy into your dreams, they will want to help turn those dreams into reality.

Second, through your planned gifts committee or another planned gifts advisory group, ask them to help identify planned gift prospects. Meet regularly, both individually and one-on-one, to:

• Identify planned gift prospects
• Rate and screen planned gift prospects
• Determine appropriate ways of approaching the prospects
• Discuss ways in which individual planned gifts might be funded
• Review funding opportunities that may be of interest to prospects

Involving centers of influence in these ways will bring your nonprofit to the forefront and multiply your efforts toward generating planned gifts.

Build a Capable Planned Gifts Committee

How many people do you have promoting planned gift opportunities or even identifying planned gift prospects on your behalf?

Regardless of your organization's size or level of fundraising sophistication, the development of a planned gifts committee can work wonders in expanding and achieving related objectives.

There is a wide range of valuable tasks planned gift committees can assume to increase the number of planned gifts being realized. Here are just a few:

1. Make personal planned gift provisions as examples to others.

2. Identify and refer the names of likely planned gift prospects from their communities or circle of acquaintances.

3. Work to introduce planned gift prospects to your organization and cultivate their interest.

4. Develop and approve policies related to planned gifts — types of gifts accepted, restrictions on planned gifts, investment policies, stewardship policies, etc.

5. Identify and establish rapport with agents of wealth — trust officers, attorneys, accountants, insurance agents and others.

6. Host receptions for those who have made planned gift provisions.

7. Identify appropriate ways of recognizing those who have made planned gifts.

Although many nonprofits form a planned gifts committee of some sort, many lack direction and drive. Work to create and nurture a can-do committee. Provide them with a job description and clear expectations.

Where to Look for Planned Gift Committee Membership

• Those who have already made planned gift provisions.
• Board members.
• Obvious planned gift prospects.
• Employees (and former employees) who have made or may make planned gift provisions.
• Agents of wealth — attorneys, trust officers, accountants, insurance agents and others.

INVOLVE VOLUNTEERS, NURTURE A PLANNED GIFTS COMMITTEE

Advisory Council Members Serve as Strong Advocates

Thirty people of various ages, professions and interests come together to serve as advocates for the Sidney Kimmel Comprehensive Cancer Center at Johns Hopkins (Baltimore, MD).

"The mission is for the (advisory council) members to be knowledgeable, informed advocates for the cancer center," Ellen Stifler, director of development, says of the 9-year-old advisory council.

Members of the elite group advocate for the organization. Some refer friends to the cancer center for care. Others share their knowledge of cancer and the center with colleagues and government officials, spearhead fundraising efforts or assist with donor cultivation and gift solicitation.

"There have been times when a particular council member has come with the director or me on a call, and therefore been an advocate for the mission of the cancer center and for the purpose of the ask," Stifler says. "That also lends a real credibility as peer to peer."

While the advisory council benefits the cancer center, Stifler says, membership on the council is mutually rewarding, as it is also a great way to steward current donors.

"It is wonderful stewardship for people who care about the cancer center's mission," Stifler says. "They learn a lot. It is very educational. Additionally, people like to be connected with the leadership of the Kimmel Cancer Center. It brings them into the family."

To create a successful and productive advisory council, remember, "The most important thing is the people you bring in," she says. "Be very careful in selecting the right people. They should be eager for new ideas, have new ideas and respect the director's plans." Additionally, "Be willing to rethink and continually work to improve the council."

Source: Ellen Stifler, Director of Development, Sidney Kimmel Comprehensive Cancer Center at Johns Hopkins, Baltimore, MD. Phone (410) 516-4262. E-mail: stifler@jhu.edu

Motivate Advisory Council Members

Ellen Stifler, director of development, Sidney Kimmel Comprehensive Cancer Center (Baltimore, MD), says she considers the cancer center's advisory council to be strong.

However, its members recently encountered a challenge, when its well-respected and well-liked director died of cancer.

"Our challenge has been to keep our council members interested and invigorated," Stifler says. "It was our goal to maintain momentum even when we all missed our former director. We added new members, and we are continually working to reinvigorate and improve the meetings and interactions."

For example, the council, which meets biannually, will now rotate meeting locations, such as meeting in the kitchen of the cancer center's new patient and family pavilion and including a private tour.

Stifler also plans to make meetings more interactive rather than show and tell. She is planning a four-member panel discussion with experts from the cancer center talking on cancer prevention and control, allowing ample time for questions and conversation.

Nurture a League of Planned Gift Ambassadors

Although it requires a significant investment of time, building a volunteer group of planned gift ambassadors can significantly increase your ability to identify, cultivate and secure additional planned gifts for your organization.

Here's a framework for building a corps of planned gift ambassadors:

1. **Develop a three-year plan that outlines goals for your ambassador program.** How many volunteers would you like in place at the end of your first year? What communities or geographic locations would be ideal for the presence of these ambassadors?

2. **Methodically begin to recruit, train and support your ambassadors.** Invite those who have already chosen to make a planned gift to serve as ambassadors. Turn to professionals (attorneys, trust officers, insurance agents) in particular communities who have an existing connection to your cause.

3. **Provide your new recruits with a position description that shows what is expected of them** — to regularly identify, research, cultivate and assist in the solicitation of planned gift prospects.

4. **Work with and support each ambassador and ambassador group as circumstances dictate.** Take an ambassador on a call. Accompany an ambassador who is willing to introduce you to a new planned gift prospect. Meet with a community's ambassador group (which may amount to two or three individuals) to review activities and plan strategies.

Even if you have only three ambassador groups with three or four members in each group by the end of year one, you will have launched a volunteer effort that will expand and enhance your efforts to market planned gifts.

Nurture a group of select individuals who will assist with identifying, cultivating, soliciting and stewarding planned gift donors.

INVOLVE VOLUNTEERS, NURTURE A PLANNED GIFTS COMMITTEE

Seek Out Ambassadors in Wealthy Neighborhoods

If your community has residential areas that represent greater wealth, work to identify existing donors from those sections to serve as centers of influence in an ongoing capacity. Whether they become part of a major gifts committee or you choose to work with each on an individual basis, these ambassadors — who already have a history of giving to your organization and believe in your mission — can help to:

1. Identify potential donors from their assigned territories.
2. Initiate research efforts, providing useful information on neighborhood prospects.
3. Make introductions and cultivate new friendships with these residents.
4. Accompany staff on solicitation calls.
5. Steward residents from their assigned areas who have made gifts to your organization.

Making the Right Connection Makes All the Difference

Nurture your major gift prospects well, and they will remember you when the opportunity to give presents itself.

Officials at Knox College (Galesburg, IL) made such a connection with alumna Elzelien Hartog, who made a gift to the college from her father's estate.

Hartog's father left money in his estate for each of his children to use to make charitable donations, says Beverly Holmes, vice president for advancement at Knox. "The donor proposed a gift to Knox; Knox proposed the specifics of how the gift might be used."

Helping nurture the connection, says Holmes, were Knox's president and his wife, who had visited Hartog and recalled her sharing that her father was an entrepreneur and businessman who valued international understanding and travel and believed the key to understanding other people was to gain an appreciation of their culture.

Every member of the development department — in fact every employee — can help to strengthen your planned gifts efforts.

Knowing this, college officials proposed creating a fund in the man's name to support overseas travel for students through Knox's overseas programs.

The alumna's $100,000 gift to the college's Center for Global Studies funded the Joseph J. Hartog Endowment for Global Studies and Scholarship. Holmes notes that if money remains in any given year, the fund may also be used to support faculty research and development that enhances the global dimension of the curriculum.

The gift opens up ongoing stewardship as it makes Hartog a member of Knox's Lincoln-Douglas Society for donors with cumulative lifetime giving of $100,000 or more. These donors are honored at a public event and presented with a keepsake representing the college's history — a set of bookends representing Abraham Lincoln and Stephen A. Douglas.

Knox College is the only remaining site of the famous Lincoln-Douglas debates of 1858. The bookends were designed and sculpted by an alumna whose interest in art was kindled by a Knox professor.

Members of the Lincoln-Douglas Society also receive an annual mailing from Knox featuring a book, written by a faculty member, that has wide appeal among the members in the society.

Source: Beverly Holmes, Vice President for Advancement, Knox College, Galesburg, IL. Phone (309) 341-7755. E-mail: bholmes@knox.edu

---

Everyone Can Assist With Your Planned Gifts Effort

The responsibility of planned gifts should not rest with one individual alone. Each member of the advancement team, in fact every employee within an organization, can assist with this ongoing effort.

Here's a sampling of the ways in which others can assist with planned giving:

- **Identify persons within your own circle of friends, relatives and contacts** who may be planned gift prospects, and share their names with your planned gifts officer.

- **Educate yourself.** Meet with the planned gifts officer to learn how you would go about making a personal planned gift. Whether you make a gift or not, you will learn more about planned gifts by exploring the possibilities.

- **Include planned gift prospects among your calls.** The planned gifts officer does not need to be the only staff member cultivating prospects. When you are on the road, take time to make calls on planned gift prospects. Be sure to first clear your visit with the planned gifts officer.

INVOLVE VOLUNTEERS, NURTURE A PLANNED GIFTS COMMITTEE

Advisory Council Focuses on Boosting Planned Gifts, Educating Community

Community Education Series Educates Public on Planned Giving

A major role the planned gift advisory council at Wentworth-Douglass Hospital & Health Foundation (Dover, NH) fulfills is educating the community about issues related to planned giving. One way the council accomplishes this is through its community education series.

Series offerings for 2011 focus on a variety of topics while engaging experts with a wide range of professional expertise, including:

- **"Charitable Planning: Doing Well by Doing Good"** with Bernie Lebs and Patrick F. Olearcek, JD, CLU, ChFC, MassMutual Financial Group

- **"How to 'Do' Estate Planning With or Without the Federal Estate Tax"** with Bruce Johnson, Johnson & Associates & Tom Levasseur, The Beacon Retirement Group

- **"How to Do More With What You Have: Leveraging your Legacy"** with Robert Boulanger, Oppenheimer & Co., Inc. & Ken Money, Money Law Offices

- **"Veteran's Benefit"** with Rich Hilow, Financial Advisor, Edward Jones

- **"College Financial Planning"** with Melanie Dupuis, CPA, CCPS, Larry Raiche & Company CPAs

- **"Get the Facts"** A Reverse Mortgage Educational Event with Tom Torr, Cochecho Elder Law Associates & Kathleen Burke, Wells Fargo Home Mortgage

- **"Guardianship and Powers of Attorney—When Kids Become the Parents"** with Stephanie Burnham, Stephanie K. Burnham & Associates

- **"Rethinking Retirement Planning"** with Tom Levasseur, The Beacon Retirement Group & Karen Zaramba, Hunter Advisor Group, A Capital L member firm

- **"Saving Employee Benefit Costs While Keeping Employees Happy"** with Mark Jacobsohn, Relayer Benefits Group, LLC

- **"Changes in Taxation Due to Current Political Environment That Impact Retirement, Investment and Planned Giving"** with Dave Verno, CPA, Leone, McDonnell & Roberts, PA

A planned gift advisory council is having a major impact on planned giving at Wentworth-Douglass Hospital & Health Foundation (Dover, NH).

According to Deborah Shelton, vice president of philanthropy & chief philanthropy officer, the foundation is slated to receive at least 50 new planned gifts, with approximately 100 donors participating in its planned giving program.

Shelton credits much of that activity to the advisory council that includes estate-planning attorneys, financial planners, benefit professionals, certified public accountants, trust officers and other allied professionals.

The council meets five times a year. Meetings begin with a half-hour open forum about the hospital, followed by a business meeting. Members are expected to assist in identifying and nurturing persons capable of making a planned gift to the foundation, support the foundation themselves through gifts to the annual appeal and attend planned meetings and workshops as their schedule permits.

The members also offer a community education series, educating the public on issues involved with planned giving (see box, left).

To further engage these valued professionals and make them feel invested in the hospital and health foundation, Shelton says, she and her staff invite them to all open houses and special events.

Source: Deborah Shelton, Vice President of Philanthropy & Chief Philanthropy Officer, Wentworth-Douglass Hospital & Health Foundation, Dover, NH. Phone (603) 740-2894. E-mail: Deborah.Shelton@wdhospital.com

Content not available in this edition

How to Get a Planned Gifts Program Up and Running, Second Edition.
Edited by Scott C. Stevenson.
© 2011 Stevenson, Inc. Published 2011 by Stevenson, Inc.

PLANNED GIFTS OPTIONS TO OFFER

Since it's not uncommon that as much as 80 percent or more of charitable planned gifts come in the form of bequests, you need not know everything about the many types of gift options available to get a program up and running. But it does make sense to develop a basic knowledge of various planned gift options. The more time you are able to devote to planned gifts, the more knowledgeable you will become about the available planned gift vehicles — and accompanying donor benefits.

Help Donors Benefit Their Heirs and Your Charity

Want to help donors benefit their children, grandchildren and your charity as well? Then suggest either of these two planned gift options:

Combination of a **testamentary charitable bequest and an irrevocable life insurance trust** — after the donor's lifetime, the charitable bequest provides the gift to the charity and a life insurance trust provides the funds needed for the donors' children or grandchildren.

Nonreversionary charitable lead trust — this gift provides income to the charitable organization followed by the means to transfer the donor's assets to heirs upon the termination of the trust. This type of planned gift is most utilized by the very wealthy since it provides no immediate benefit to the donor or the donor's family.

These two types of planned gifts allow donors to fulfill philanthropic goals and still transfer wealth to their children and grandchildren.

Your job as a planned gifts officer is two-fold: 1) to generate planned gifts for your nonprofit and 2) to look out for the best interests of those with whom you communicate.

Don't Underestimate the Advantages of Bequests

In spite of the many planned gift arrangements available to donors (e.g., charitable annuities, unitrusts, annuity trusts, lead gifts and more), bequests remain the most popular method, and for good reason:

Bequests continue to be the most popular planned gifts made.

- As long as an individual has a will, bequests are simple gifts for donors to establish.

- Unlike some planned gifts, donors retain control of their assets during their lifetimes.

- Bequests can be promoted by a charity with a minimum amount of cost and resources.

- Bequests qualify for an estate tax charitable deduction.

> According to *Giving USA 2010:*
>
> - Estimated charitable bequests of $23.8 billion represented 9.1 percent of total estimated charitable giving for 2010.

- To the donor's advantage, one bequest can benefit multiple charities.

Understand Bequest Types

Even if you're not a planned giving expert, it's important that you know the various types of bequests donors can make to your charity, especially since the bequest is, by far, the most popular type of planned gift made.

Here's the lineup:

Understand the differences that exist between these types of bequests.

Specific bequest — The donor bequeaths a certain amount of cash or specific assets to the charity.

Residual bequest — Bequest of all or a portion of the remainder or residue of a donor's estate after specific and other bequests have been distributed.

Percentage bequest — The charity receives a certain percentage of the donor's estate or of another asset.

Contingent bequest — The charity receives the estate if others named in the will are not living at the time of the donor's death. Example: "I give all the rest, residue and remainder of my real and personal estate to my husband, (name), if he survives me; if not, then 50 percent in equal shares to my children who survive me and 50 percent to (name of charity)."

PLANNED GIFTS OPTIONS TO OFFER

Suggest Residual Bequests as One Giving Option

As you cover the topic of charitable bequests with planned gift prospects, don't forget to suggest the residual bequest as one option.

Residual bequests are gifts of the remainder of an estate after all specific bequests have been distributed.

When combined with specific bequests, residual bequests allow the donor to ensure friends and relatives are adequately provided for, while still making a gift to charity.

Unrestricted Residual Bequest

I give (Name of Nonprofit, Address)), (_____ percent of the residue of my estate) or (the sum of $_____), to be used by (Name of Nonprofit), wherever the needs and opportunities are greatest.

Consider Charitable Gift Annuity Advantages

Don't overlook the charitable gift annuity as a viable planned gift option this year. Here's why:

1. Recent retirees who choose to switch some stocks into fixed income arrangements can minimize capital gains and receive deductions as well.

2. They can dip into principal without fear of running out of savings.

3. Annuity payments are partly tax free during a recipient's life expectancy.

4. Charitable deductions benefit donors, especially those planning a Roth IRA conversion this year.

5. Baby boomers can replenish retirement nest eggs depleted during the recession by arranging deferred payment gift annuities.

Source: The Estate Planner, American Institute for Cancer Research, Washington, D.C. Website: www.aicr.org

Market Charitable Gift Annuities Aggressively

What is your organization doing to market charitable gift annuities as an attractive planned gift?

The charitable gift annuity allows the donor to convey cash, securities or other property to your charity and, in return, receive multiple benefits during the donor's lifetime (e.g., tax deduction, capital gains savings, annual income for the donor and another named individual during their lifetimes).

This planned gift usually makes the most sense for elderly donor-annuitants who are philanthropically motivated.

Use these and other procedures to encourage your constituents to establish charitable gift annuities:

Tip: Notify past gift annuity donors to announce annuity payout rate hikes and to encourage repeat gifts.

Increasing numbers of planned gift websites include a calculator that allows visitors to determine payout rates and deductions.

1. Offer examples of how a charitable gift annuity might work during face-to-face visits, through direct mail and on your website. Example: Central Park Conservancy (New York, NY) — www.centralparknyc.org/support/plannedgiving/charitablegiftannuities

2. Invite prospects to complete a simple form that will allow them to calculate how a charitable gift annuity would work for them based on their ages, gift amount and type of gift. Example: Lucile Packard Foundation for Children's Health (Palo Alto, CA) — www.lpfch.planyourgift.org/illustration.php

PLANNED GIFTS OPTIONS TO OFFER

For Those Considering Restricted Bequests...

Encourage donors — especially those considering restricted planned gifts — to consult with your charity prior to making final estate planning decisions to help guarantee the gifts are used as they intend.

Anyone making a restricted planned gift unbeknownst to the charity runs the risk of: 1) the bequest being disqualified from the estate tax charitable deduction or 2) the charity rejecting the gift because of the nature of the restriction.

At the least, donors should consider a conditional bequest that would fail upon the occurrence or nonoccurrence of some event. A conditional bequest remains tax deductible if, at time of bequestor's death, the likelihood of the bequest failing is so remote as to be negligible.

Suggest Life Insurance as a Gift Option

Many of your constituents believe they're not in a position to make a major gift. But if they own one or more life insurance policies, they can make a significant contribution. This is an especially appropriate gift if the donor considers the policy's protection to be less important than it once was.

Include articles, such as the example shown here, in various publications to illustrate how easily and painlessly life insurance can be converted into a major gift.

Gift a Life Insurance Policy

If you have determined you no longer need a life insurance policy or its cash value, you have two gifting options: 1) You can make a charity the beneficiary of the policy; or 2) you can gift the ownership of the policy to a favorite charity.

The policy owner, generally the insured or his/her spouse, has the right to change the beneficiary to a charity. Then at the insured's death, the life insurance is paid to the charity. As policy owner, the life insurance benefits are included in your taxable estate; however, this will be offset by the charitable deduction. By informing the charity of its status as beneficiary, you will have the opportunity to direct the use of the gift (annual fund, endowment or a special project). With this option, you will be required to continue to pay the premiums unless you also select a paid-up policy option.

The second option includes gifting ownership of the policy to a charity. You receive a charitable deduction for the cash value of the policy and continue to make a charitable contribution in the amount of the premium to offset its costs.

As the owner, the charity also has the option to terminate the policy and accept the cash value. Given the tax status of the charity, it will pay no income tax on the cash value, even if some portion is determined to be taxable.

Distinguish Life Insurance Gift Options

Life insurance can permit a donor to make a substantial gift for a relatively modest cost. It's sometimes referred to as an affordable way to make a major gift.

There are two basic ways to gift an insurance policy:

The charity as beneficiary only — The donor retains ownership of the policy and has access to the policy's cash value. Since the donor retains ownership of the life insurance policy, no income tax deduction is allowed for the value of the policy upon designation of the charitable organization as the beneficiary or for subsequent premium payments. However, the donor's estate will be entitled to an estate tax deduction.

The charity as both owner and beneficiary — A donor who wishes more immediate tax benefits may prefer the irrevocable assignment of an insurance policy to the charity. The donor is allowed an immediate federal income tax deduction for the lesser of the policy's fair market value or the net premiums paid. The donor can take income tax deductions on contributions made directly to the charity when paying subsequent premiums.

PLANNED GIFT OPTIONS TO OFFER

Soliciting Life Insurance Gifts

Accepting gifts of life insurance policies can be lucrative, but it can also be problematic, depending on how the gift is made, says Adam Aptowitzer, a lawyer with Drache Aptowitzer (Ottawa, Ontario, Canada).

"If the individual names the charity as beneficiary, that is easy and the nonprofit typically doesn't know about the gift until the donor's death," Aptowitzer says. But if the person donates a policy while he/she is living, the nonprofit must deal with the premium, he says. "If the nonprofit can't pay the premium, the donation might be worthless, although the nonprofit could secure a donation of the premium until the donor dies."

A major advantage of life insurance policies as gifts, he says, is that they can have a large payout for a small investment.

One disadvantage, says Aptowitzer, is the potential risk to a nonprofit's reputation related to accepting such gifts from donors who may later realize they still need the policy (and may be uninsurable by then); or there are dependents left with no means of support other than the donated policy.

Paula Straub, president, Save Gains Tax LLC (San Marcos, CA), former investment advisor representative and current insurance agent, agrees that in the right circumstances, gifts of life insurance policies can be advantageous for nonprofits. However, she says, in today's cash-strapped nonprofit environment, large monthly premiums can strain a nonprofit's resources.

Alternatives to turning away a gift based on inability to pay the premium are to ask the donor to sell the policy to a life settlement company and donate cash proceeds to the nonprofit, or for the nonprofit to accept the gift and sell it to a life settlement company itself, says Straub.

Here is a sampling of life settlement companies:

- The Life Settlement Company of America (www.lscoa.com)
- IMS Associates (www.imssettlements.com)
- Integrity Capital Partners (www.integrityp.com)
- Life Policy Group (www.lifepolicygroup.com)

Sources: Adam Aptowitzer, Lawyer, Drache Aptowitzer, Ottawa, Ontario, Canada.
Phone (613) 237-3300. E-mail: adamapt@drache.ca
Paula Straub, President, Save Gains Tax LLC, San Marcos, CA.
Phone (760) 917-0858. E-mail: savegainstax@gmail.com

Ask Donors to Consider a Gift of Life Insurance

A gift of life insurance is a great way for a donor to make a substantial gift using an asset they no longer need. Here are some ways donors can make a gift of life insurance, and the donor benefits of each:

- **Name the charity as beneficiary.** The donor receives an estate tax deduction, but no tax benefit during his or her lifetime since the gift is revocable.

- **Donate a paid-up policy, naming the charity as beneficiary, and transferring the ownership to the charity.** Made in this way, the gift is irrevocable, so the donor is eligible for an immediate income tax deduction each year for up to 50 percent of their adjusted gross income. Any excess can be carried forward for up to five additional years.

- **Donate a new or partially paid policy.** The donor receives a deduction approximately equal to the policy's current value, along with additional deductions for continuing to pay the premiums.

Life Estate Gift Basics

What is a life estate gift? A life estate gift is a restricted gift of property (a home, vacation home, rental property, section of land, etc.) made to a charity in which the donor retains the rights to the property during his or her lifetime and/or the lifetime of a family member (spouse, child, etc.).

How does a life estate gift work? The donor retains the right to use, improve and/or make money from the property during his/her lifetime or the lifetime of his or her beneficiary. Once the donor and his or her beneficiary dies, the property goes to the charity.

What are the donor benefits of a life estate gift? Although the donor and his or her beneficiary retain the rights to the property until their deaths, the donor receives an immediate income tax deduction for part of the property's value. Since the property won't be in the donor's estate when he/she dies, the estate could also save taxes and probate costs. If the donor gives up the property during his/her lifetime, he/she can receive additional tax benefits at that time. (The value of the tax deduction depends on the value of the land and the age of the donor.)

PLANNED GIFT OPTIONS TO OFFER

Retained Life Estate Agreements Offer Many Advantages

Gifts of retained life estate — where a donor deeds property to a charity while retaining the right to use it during his/her lifetime — offer many advantages, particularly if a donor has no natural heirs or has numerous heirs scattered across the country, says Donna Roseman David, senior gift planning officer, Hartford Foundation for Public Giving (Hartford, CT).

Roseman David discusses elements that should be part of retained life estate agreements, based on the sample offered by the Hartford Foundation (right):

1. **Donor's right of usage.** Use of the property through the end of one's life is one primary benefit to the donor, says Roseman David. The right also allows charities to receive larger gifts than the donor might otherwise be able to make.

2. **Donor responsibilities.** Properly structured agreements protect the charity from ongoing and upkeep expenses like taxes, utilities and assessments.

3. **Property damage.** This clause obliges the donor to assume repair costs or split insurance payments with the charity. Roseman David says donors usually provide certification of insurance and premium payment by adding the charity as an additional insured party on the policy, ensuring the organization receives copies of all relevant paperwork.

4. **Indemnity.** This clause provides further protection against cost and damages.

5. **Property inspection.** A gift of retained life estate is an asset, and organizations have a responsibility to protect their assets. Because every property and donor is different, she suggests using a professional inspection service prior to accepting the gift to determine the most appropriate type and frequency of inspection.

6. **Property modification.** This clause protects both the donor's right to improve the property and the charity's right to maintain the value of its asset.

7. **Amendment.** While a gift of remainder interest must be made irrevocably to provide the donor with tax advantages, an amendment clause offers both parties a way to refine arrangements regarding inspection, maintenance and such.

Source: Donna Roseman David, Senior Gift Planning Officer, Hartford Foundation for Public Giving, Hartford, CT. Phone (860) 548-1888. E-mail: Ddavid@hfpg.org

Content not available in this edition

PLANNED GIFT OPTIONS TO OFFER

Don't Overlook the Profitable Possibilities of Retained Life Estate Gifts

Content not available in this edition

Every real estate gift is uniquely challenging, says Phillip Purcell, vice president of planned giving and endowment stewardship, Ball State University Foundation (Muncie, IN.)

Purcell answers questions and shares insights on a class of donations known as retained life estate (RLE) gifts, which the planned giving expert says is a gift option nonprofit organizations often overlook:

What is a retained life estate gift?

"It's an irrevocable gift of the remainder interest in a donor's personal residence or farm. The donor keeps a life estate, retains the right to live on and use it during his or her lifetime, and on death it passes to the charitable institution (see illustration)."

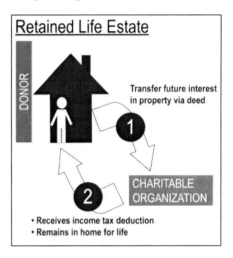

Retained Life Estate

DONOR

Transfer future interest in property via deed

1

2

CHARITABLE ORGANIZATION

• Receives income tax deduction
• Remains in home for life

How does that differ from bequeathing a home in a will?

"Revocability is one of the big differences. Bequests are revocable, and some people like the flexibility this offers. They like having more control over the home or farm, and being able to sell it should they need the cash. RLE gifts are irrevocable and less flexible in some ways, but offer many advantages as well."

What are some of these advantages?

"Primarily tax benefits. Because the gift is irrevocable, the donor can take an income tax charitable deduction (based on their age and the value of the property) in the year the gift is made, rather than waiting until the end of life. The transfer is not subject to capital gains tax, and the property passes free of federal estate tax as long as the life estate is left to a charitable institution.

"From the charity's perspective, a major benefit is the absence of probate. Because RLE is irrevocable, it is not subject to probate and therefore escapes the fees and delays associated with that process."

When do gifts of RLE make the most sense?

"There are two primary scenarios. The first is when the charity wants to use the land itself, for expanding a campus or building a camp for kids or something like that. The second involves land, which the charity doesn't want to use, but which is valuable and likely to become more valuable over time — real estate like farmland, property in the path of development or land in resort or vacation areas.

"In either situation, a gift of RLE allows the donor to retain use of the property while still ensuring it ends up in the hands of the charity."

Source: Philip Purcell, Vice President for Planned Giving and Endowment Stewardship, Ball State University Foundation, Muncie, IN. Phone (765) 285-8312. E-mail: ppurcell@bsu.edu

PLANNED GIFT OPTIONS TO OFFER

If someone wants to make a substantial charitable gift, split-interest charitable techniques allow the donor to make the gift today while retaining an interest in the property and enjoying both immediate and long-term tax benefits.

What's a Split-interest Gift?

What is it? A split-interest gift is a charitable gift in which the donor or his or her beneficiaries split the benefits with a charity.

What types of gifts are considered split-interest gifts? Charitable gift annuities, charitable lead trusts, life estate agreements, pooled income funds and charitable remainder trusts.

How does a split-interest gift work? It depends on the type of split-interest gift. For example, for a charitable remainder trust, the donor contributes the asset to a charity and receives income tax savings and income from the trust for a certain number of years or for life. When the donor dies, the charity receives the asset.

What are the donor benefits of a split-interest gift? Tax savings and the ability to make a gift to a charity while retaining some of the benefits of the asset.

Suggest Deferred Payment Gift Annuity to Younger Crowd

Your younger planned gift prospects — say, those persons ages 40 to 60 — may wish to consider a deferred payment gift annuity as a planned gift option, especially if they have a high income, need to benefit now from a current tax deduction and wish to add to future retirement income.

The deferred payment gift annuity involves the current transfer of cash or marketable securities, in exchange for which the nonprofit agrees to pay the donor an annuity starting at some future date (at least one year after the date of the gift). The gift can consist of a single transfer, a series of transfers, or periodic transfers to the plan in high-income years.

The donor realizes an immediate charitable deduction for the gift portion of each transfer to the deferred gift-annuity plan. A portion of each annuity payment, when the payments begin, will be a tax-free return of principal over the life expectancy of the annuitant.

When appreciated, long-term, capital gain securities are transferred, any reportable capital gain is spread over the donor-annuitant's life expectancy.

A deferred payment gift annuity may be established for the benefit of one or two individual annuitants, and the donor need not be one.

Deferred Payment Gift Annuity Features, Benefits

- Donors receive payments at least annually once they begin.
- Donor's fixed-dollar income is guaranteed for life.
- Income is based on age of the beneficiaries and length of deferment until payments begin.
- A charitable deduction is allowed immediately for the present value of donor's gift.
- A portion of the income is tax-free over the expected life of the gift annuity.
- The donor benefits from favorable capital gains treatment and deferral of capital gains until the date the annuity begins if the annuity is funded with appreciated assets.
- Deferred payment gift annuities help reduce the donor's estate tax and probate costs.

Planned Gift Basics: Stepped Charitable Gift Annuity

A charitable gift annuity is a contract between a donor and charity stating that, in exchange for the donor's gift, the charity agrees to pay the donor a fixed dollar amount annually for life. A stepped annuity can be structured with income steadily increasing for a period of years based on a predetermined schedule.

Appeal to Donors' Hearts

Although planned gift donors will weigh the benefits of various types of gifts — tax savings, helping loved ones and more — the primary motivation for making any planned gift will be driven by the heart — the desire to help, to make a positive difference and to leave a legacy.

It's important to recognize the roles that both head and heart play in the realization of planned gifts.

PLANNED GIFT OPTIONS TO OFFER

Are You Ready for CGAs?

Charitable gift annuities (CGAs) — binding financial agreements between a nonprofit and a major donor — can be a great way to acquire large-scale donations. Yet, only a small percentage of nonprofits in the United States offer CGAs to major donors because of the planning and paperwork involved.

How do you know if your nonprofit is prepared to take on the added risk, responsibility — and reward — CGAs bring?

S.C. Chase Adams, managing director of Adams Associates (Ft. Lauderdale, FL), a law firm specializing in fundraising and estate preservation strategies, suggests referencing your organization's strengths and weaknesses against this five-point checklist:

1. **Are your books impeccable?** In a CGA with a donor, your organization is legally responsible for investing the donor's money in such a way as to guarantee payments to the donor, possibly for decades, requiring extra — and precise — accounting.

2. **How solid is your organization's long-term outlook?** With CGAs, nonprofits receive full ownership of the gift upon the donor's death. This is, of course, not something you can plan for, so the rest of your organization's long-term prospects need to be equally strong in the interim.

3. **What staff resources can you allocate or increase for the sake of CGAs?** The time, energy and expense of administering a CGA program can be onerous and expensive, says Adams. Tasks include record-keeping for each CGA account and a lengthy registration process each state requires before a nonprofit can enter into CGAs.

4. **What assets do you already have?** In some states, a nonprofit must pledge a percentage of assets as collateral to insure the donor's payments. Other states require that a nonprofit pledge all of its assets to qualify for CGA status.

5. **How much can you afford to financially invest in administering CGAs?** Although the adage usually applies to the for-profit sector, spending money to make money definitely applies to any nonprofit organization seeking CGAs.

Source: S.C. Chase Adams, Managing Director, Adams Associates, Fort Lauderdale, FL.
Phone (954) 449-4970. E-mail: info@chaseadams.net. Website: www.financialarchitect.com

Charitable gift annuities are one way middle-level donors can make major, even transformational, gifts.

MEETING ONE-ON-ONE

Although planning, goal setting and personal correspondence with planned gift prospects is important, there is nothing as important as face-to-face visits. That's where the real relationship building takes place. This chapter examines some key aspects of what can and should take place during those one-on-one meetings.

Build Donor Relationships That Last

Long-term relationships require putting the donor at the center of everything you do, according to author and consultant Simone Joyaux.

Development officers are fond of declaring that fundraising is all about relationships, but all too often that platitude is built on mistaken assumptions, says Simone Joyaux, author and principle of Joyaux Associates (Foster, RI): "Numerous gift officers and board members think they are supposed to solicit wealthy friends or acquaintances — regardless of whether they care about the organization's cause — simply because they share a personal or professional relationship. This can strain friendships and is not a sustainable approach to fundraising. The relationship has to be with the organization itself to last."

The key to building lasting relationships is putting the donor at the center of everything you do, says Joyaux. To do this, she suggests four steps:

1. **Develop a donor-centered corporate culture.** Being donor-centered does not conflict with being mission-centered; successful organizations can and should be both.

2. **Get to know your donors.** Learning your supporters' interests (and disinterests) is central to maintaining a donor-focused attitude, says Joyaux. Seek to understand the motivations and aspirations of the most loyal donors — regardless of gift size.

3. **Produce donor-centered communications.** Fundraisers need to put away the academic writing they used in college and embrace the principles of journalism, says Joyaux. "Read books and articles on marketing communication and focus on your audience. Don't write about your organization and its programs, write about your donors and what they accomplish through your organization and its programs."

4. **Create extraordinary experiences.** Engage and involve your major donors. Have a board member call and thank donors for their gifts — without an additional request. Ask why they chose to support your organization and use the story.

Source: Simone Joyaux, Principle, Joyaux Associates, Foster, RI. Phone (401) 397-2534. E-mail: spjoyaux@aol.com. Website: www.simonejoyaux.com

Content not available in this edition

Ways to Suggest A Charitable Bequest

To broach the topic of inviting individuals to consider a charitable bequest, point out reasons for having a will, such as:

- Naming individuals and organizations to receive your assets.

- Specifying how they are to receive those assets.

- Saving taxes for beneficiaries.

- Reducing expenses of settling your estate.

MEETING ONE-ON-ONE

Perfect the Art of Solicitation Small Talk

Going into a meeting with a potential donor requires plenty of preparation — and that includes preparing off-topic subjects to talk about at the start of the meeting.

"Small talk is about having knowledge of the prospect," says Jerry Smith, founder of the development consulting firm, J.F. Smith Group (Auburn, AL). Small talk, therefore, is just as important as knowing about the prospect's financial capabilities. The difference is that your prospect is much more likely to want to discuss family, hobbies and interests than stock portfolios and bank accounts.

Every solicitation meeting should begin with small talk that is off the topic of the meeting's purpose, Smith says. "When I first started in this business, I jumped right into my presentation, which isn't very good," he says. "Small talk is really important because it's an ice breaker, and because people like to talk about themselves."

While people may think the art of small talk is a natural talent, Smith insists it is a skill set you must acquire.

The most basic information to arm yourself with for successful small talk includes the donor's marital status, the occupations of the donor and his/her spouse and where both work (if applicable), children's names and their school grades.

A very easy small-talk question, Smith says, is something like, "I know Mary's in the fifth grade. How's the fifth grade going for Mary?"

To get background information on prospects, Smith says, do an online search using google.com or other search engine.

Another easy, effective way to begin small talk is to simply notice your surroundings, especially since solicitations tend to take place in the potential donor's home or office. What are people doing in the framed photos you see? Even if they are doing something you know nothing about — say playing golf — you can always ask, "How long have you played golf?" That sort of question doesn't require that you have any personal knowledge of golf to get a conversation going.

And if all else fails, Smith says, there is one, surefire question you can ask that anyone would love to answer: "Tell me, how did you get to where you are today?"

Source: Jerry Smith, Founder, J.F. Smith Group, Auburn, AL. E-mail: jerrysmith@jfsg.com. Website: www.jfsg.com

> *"Small talk" is anything but small. Establishing a good rapport with prospects is key to an effective solicitation.*

When Planned Gift Prospects Live Far Away

Do you have planned gift prospects who live far from your institution or agency? Most organizations do — alumni, former residents of a community, chapter members and others.

Whether such individuals have confirmed their intent to include your charity in their estate plans or it may be possible that they will do so at some time, how do you cultivate a relationship and maintain their interest from such a distance?

Here are some strategies for stewarding long-distance planned gift prospects:

Establish a tickler system. Send regular messages from your institution at irregular intervals. Create a monthly reminder of who should receive a phone call, a birthday or anniversary card, or other appropriate (but not contrived) communications.

Send a videotape. Produce a once-a-year video — using an inexpensive camcorder to keep expenses down, if necessary — that can be distributed to all faraway prospects. Provide a narrated tour of your facility; interview some employees or those served by your organization; produce a nostalgic "I remember when" video for older prospects.

Send "there's no place like home" reminders. For former residents of your area, send reminders of their hometown links — products produced in your community/state, books/periodicals with regional flavor or news clippings from your local newspaper.

Include personal notes with each planned gifts newsletter. If you produce a quarterly planned gifts newsletter, include an occasional personal note for some of your faraway clients to personalize the mailing.

> *Don't let geographic distance come between you and individuals who want to support the mission of your organization.*

MEETING ONE-ON-ONE

Get Donors to Say 'Yes' With These Simple Words

The right words can have a significant impact in conversations with current and potential donors, says Kevin Hogan (Eden Prairie, MN), author of the book, "The Psychology of Persuasion: How to Persuade Others to Your Way of Thinking."

In conversations, Hogan says, certain words can cause "yes" to happen.

Here, he explains why certain words prompt individuals to respond to a request with a "yes" instead of a "no". Increase your chance of fundraising success by working these words into your solicitations:

Because

"Remember when you were a kid and your mother told you to clean your room?" says Hogan. "You said, 'Why?' and she said, 'Because I said so,' and you cleaned your room. You are literally programmed to do what a person asks after he says 'because.'" For example, "We would appreciate having your support because it will show the community how important this project is to the people we serve."

Imagine

"In order to create resistance-free communication, don't obligate the person to the task, simply ask them to imagine it," says Hogan. "No one objects because you aren't asking them to take an action, but rather, to watch a movie in their mind." For example: "Just imagine the Kevin Hogan Center for Cancer Research. Wouldn't that be wonderful?"

Now

"'Now' triggers a childhood-programmed piece of code to do what you're asked. Your mother told you to go to bed, you resisted, she said, 'Now,' and you went. 'Now' is a punctuation mark, but the more softly it comes across in a solicitation, the more likely the person will be to comply with the request." For example, "Our dream, which we hope you can fulfill, is that you make your gift now, so we can count you among our pace-setting donors."

Don't

"(The word) 'don't' directs a person's behavior based on their inborn need to rebel against what they're not supposed to do," he says. "People don't like to have choices removed. When you tell a child, 'Don't touch the TV,' that's the thing they'll touch." For example, "Don't feel obligated to commit to the gift today."

Person's Name

"Nothing matters more to a person than his or her name," says Hogan. "Use it once, at the beginning. When you use a person's name once, the rapport value goes high, high, high. Use it a second time and it levels off. As you use it a third, fourth, fifth and sixth time, the rapport value goes way down. If you overuse it, people will feel as if they're being manipulated." For example: "Hi John, great to see you. I'm excited to tell you about the campaign."

Source: Kevin Hogan, International Consultant, Speaker, Corporate Trainer & Author, Eden Prairie, MN. Phone (612) 616-0732. E-mail: Kevin@kevinhogan.com. Website: www.kevinhogan.com

Avoid Asking 'How Much?'

When you discover someone has included your charity in estate plans, avoid the temptation to ask how much is being directed to your cause. Such a question may offend many donors.

Here's another approach to try: Gently ask if they have an intended use for the gift once it is given. This will often evolve into conversations that eventually get at the amount of the planned gift without having to ask directly and risk causing hard feelings.

Endowment Size	
Charity A	$13 million
Charity B	$19 million
Charity C	$6.5 million
Charity D	$8 million
Our Charity	$4.4 million

Use a chart similar to this to compare your charity's endowment size to other benchmark charities.

Marketing Planned Gifts

- As you assist planned gift prospects, develop proposals based on what's best for them — those that will minimize income subject to taxes and maximize deductions that reduce their taxable income.

MEETING ONE-ON-ONE

Learn How to 'Listen the Gift'

Many fundraisers fail to work on two of the most important factors in securing major gifts — probing and listening — says fundraising consultant Jerold Panas of Jerold Panas, Linzy & Partners (Chicago, IL).

"If you do all the talking, you are in the spotlight, (and) it is your agenda, not the donor's," he says. "As a result, you won't learn anything new about the prospective donor."

But if you listen 75 percent of the time and talk 25 percent of the time, Panas says, "You don't have to even ask for the gift. You will 'listen' the gift. By listening carefully, you will know precisely what will motivate the prospective donor and the amount you should ask for."

Listening is one skill that can be taught and learned, Panas says. He has developed an instrument called "Listen the Gift: A Guide to Effective Listening," that helps people measure their effectiveness in listening. The four-page, 58-question tool (shown in part, here) includes sections on concentration, relationship building and personal concerns.

For example, the instrument asks persons to gauge their listening quotient based on statements such as:

- ❑ Concentration: "When I talk with someone, I have a better recollection of what they said as opposed to what I said."

- ❑ Relationship building: "I attempt to gather more information about the other person by asking questions."

- ❑ Personal concerns: "I care greatly about people and those I meet and talk with, and they can sense that in my listening."

Persons rank their listening skills on a rating scale from 5 (always) to -2 (never). The total points tell the person their "listening quotient" from "Outstanding — You're great!" to "Active listening is an acquired talent — You should make an effort to improve your skills."

Panas uses this instrument in his workshops, asking attendees to review it and then using it to talk about how to improve listening skills. Individuals can also fill it out themselves and then ask a colleague, supervisor or spouse to fill it out for them and compare the results.

The guide is also a valuable staff exercise, says Panas, who says staff can take the test and then talk about the results to determine where they excel and where there may be room for them to improve listening skills and, ultimately, boost their ability to raise funds.

Source: Jerold Panas, Jerold Panas, Linzy & Partners, Chicago, IL. Phone (312) 222-1212. E-mail: ideas@panaslinzy.com. Website: www.jeroldpanas.com

Content not available in this edition

MEETING ONE-ON-ONE

Point Out All Benefits of Income-producing Gifts

Always put yourself in the shoes of the planned gift prospect. What benefits would you seek?

Whether you're discussing a charitable gift annuity, charitable remainder unitrust or some other income-producing planned gift, leave no stone unturned in pointing out donor benefits. Those benefits may include:

- Annual income for the donor and beneficiary.

- Improved earning potential of low-yielding assets.

- Bypassing realized capital gains on gifts of appreciated assets.

- Immediate federal income tax deduction.

- Estate tax savings.

- Expert management and investment diversification from your charity's investment manager.

- Creating a lasting legacy for the charity and those it serves.

- Membership in your exclusive planned gifts club or society.

Hold a Briefing Meeting for Your Solicitation Team

There's nothing worse than watching a nervous person make a speech — except, perhaps, watching a nervous person make a solicitation, says David Phillips, president and CEO of Custom Development Solutions, Inc. (Mt. Pleasant, SC).

"Stammering, stuttering and apologizing are a disaster in the making," Phillips says. "You need a solicitor who will unashamedly look a donor in the face and calmly, clearly and articulately ask for their support. And you get that by making sure people feel well-rehearsed and well-prepared."

To achieve such preparation, Phillips advocates convening a formal meeting of all solicitors (he recommends at least two), plus any related development officers and outside fundraising counsel. The aim of the meeting is to choreograph, point by point, what issues will be stressed, in what order, and by whom. Deciding who will make the ask is central, but Phillips says to also put thought into how you will introduce and position the request.

The briefing can serve different purposes with different personnel, says Phillips. For teams with less-experienced members, it presents an opportunity to assess capacity and give extra coaching. For long-standing teams, it creates a space for brainstorming and focused review of project details and prospect history and information.

A natural companion to the briefing meeting is a formal debriefing held as soon as possible after the call, says Phillips. Considering questions like how the call went, whether the request was made properly, what can be done to effect the most positive response and what upcoming action steps will provide a mechanism to establish ongoing learning and continuous improvement.

Source: David Phillips, President and CEO, Custom Development Solutions, Inc., Mt. Pleasant, SC. Phone (800) 761-3833. E-mail: dgp@cdsfunds.com. Website: www.cdsfunds.com

Focus Preparation on Four Possible Solicitation Replies

Inexperienced development officers often agonize over problematic solicitation scenarios. To lessen that anxiety, explain that virtually all responses fall into four categories, says David Phillips, president and CEO of Custom Development Solutions, Inc. (Mt. Pleasant, SC):

"A prospect can say, 'Yes,' and you start talking details. A prospect can say, 'No, it's not for me,' and that is pretty much that. A prospect can say, 'Wow, that's a significant commitment. I'll need some time to think about it.' This is the most common response and leads to a follow-up meeting.

"Finally, a prospect can say something like 'I can't do $100,000, but I might be able to do $50,000.' This is the most complicated response, because you then need to figure out whether you will accept that amount or suggest a higher figure."

Phillips says that figuring out which category any given scenario falls into can help volunteers or new solicitors feel more comfortable and prepared.

MEETING ONE-ON-ONE

Ask Donors to Complete an Intention Form

At the Fred Hutchinson Cancer Research Center (Seattle, WA), an intention form allows planned giving donors to clearly communicate various aspects of their plans in writing, says Lynette A. Klein, senior director of planned giving.

The form is used to gather contact information, gift details, recognition options and options for memorial recognition, as well as the specific amount or percentage of the planned gift (and estimated amount, if applicable).

"A lot of donors include a percentage of what they are donating to a charity or charities in their will," Klein says, "and the value of that percentage can change a lot from the time they fill it out until the gift is made, so many do not include the estimated amount."

The form is available online and in print form, Klein says, noting that while few people currently fill it out online, center officials hope to increase that number as online giving of planned gifts increases.

The print form, shown here, is a four-panel document used by the center's front-line fundraisers and given to anyone seeking information about planned gifts.

"The form is useful in a couple ways," she says. "It tells donors about the type of information that is helpful for us to know even if they don't fill it out. Others fill it out, which provides us with information that allows us to have a written confirmation of how a donor wishes their gift to be recognized during their lifetime."

The form's primary value to the center, says Klein, is that it allows them to talk to the donor about their recognition options and their wishes for how the gift is used: "I like the form because it lists different recognition options that we can look at with the donor and discuss with them."

Source: Lynette A. Klein, Senior Director of Planned Giving, Fred Hutchinson Cancer Research Center, Seattle, WA. Phone (206) 667-2754. E-mail: lklein@fhcrc.org

Legacy Partners
in Research

Intention Form

Content not available in this edition

Persons considering planned gifts to the Fred Hutchinson Cancer Research Center (Seattle, WA) can complete this intention form. See the online version at: www.fhcrc. org/donating/indiv/planned/ partnerintent.html.

MEETING ONE-ON-ONE

Follow Up Visits With a Summary Letter

Each face-to-face visit you have with a planned gift prospect is important. You will no doubt have some objective in mind each time you meet with a prospect — introduction, cultivation, solicitation or stewardship.

Following each visit, it's important to send a letter summarizing your meeting, especially since many aspects of planned gifts can be more technical and unique to the type of gift being considered,: the gift amount, the age of the donor(s) and more.

A follow-up letter allows you to reiterate key discussion points and suggest next steps in formalizing a planned gift. Such a letter also helps to reflect a higher level of professionalism.

The generic letter shown here illustrates how a follow-up letter might read depending on the nature of your visit, what's being discussed and the unique characteristics of the individual with whom you are meeting.

Always follow up every visit with a letter or handwritten note.

XYZ Nonprofit

Dear Frank:

As always, it was a pleasure to have met with you this past week. I always enjoy our visits and have such great respect for you.

I thought it might be helpful to summarize our conversation as you consider the benefits of establishing a charitable gift annuity for XYZ Nonprofit.

Based on your age of 70, you could establish a charitable gift annuity that pays an annuity rate of 6.5 percent. In exchange for a cash gift of $10,000, XYZ Nonprofit will provide you with an annuity of $650 per year for the remainder of your lifetime. Of that $650, $280.15 will be treated as ordinary income and the remaining $369.85 as tax-free income (until year 2021). In addition, you can claim a current federal charitable income tax deduction of $4,118.47.

Also as we discussed, instead of using cash to fund your gift annuity, you could fund it with appreciated stock and receive additional tax benefits. By funding the gift annuity with stock that has appreciated in value and that has been owned for longer than one year, you would significantly reduce the federal and state capital gains taxes that would have incurred had you sold the stock yourself.

I'm assuming you may have additional questions about this type of gift so I'll plan to get in touch in a couple of weeks to set another time for us to get together and chat more about it.

Thanks again, Frank, for meeting with me and weighing the benefits — to you and to XZY Nonprofit — of establishing a charitable gift annuity.

Sincerely,

Robert Griffin
Planned Gifts Director

Planned Gift Officers Tips

- Initiate a discussion by asking: "For what would you like to be remembered?"

- Close each conversation by asking: "Have you considered us with gifts in your will?"

How to Get a Planned Gifts Program Up and Running, Second Edition.
Edited by Scott C. Stevenson.
© 2011 Stevenson, Inc. Published 2011 by Stevenson, Inc.

PLANNED GIFTS NEWSLETTER & OTHER PRINTED COMMUNICATIONS

Printed communications — including a regularly published planned gifts newsletter — will help to build awareness of your planned gifts program and help to cultivate donor interest. These printed communications can also help to steward existing donors and serve to educate as well. Following are several ideas you may want to consider in your planned gifts newsletter and/or other correspondence.

Five Reasons to Distribute a Planned Gifts Newsletter

Ever wonder if the cost of a planned gifts newsletter is worth it? Here are five reasons why it pays to distribute a planned gifts newsletter to select prospects:

1. Those on your mailing list become increasingly knowledgable about how different types of charitable gifts work and the benefits of each.

2. Regular communication helps position your charity in the minds of those who receive it.

3. Real life examples and illustrations help readers more fully understand the impact of what their own planned gifts might accomplish.

4. The newsletters offer an additional avenue for recognizing those who have made planned gift commitments.

5. By including a return "bounce back" in every issue of your planned gifts newsletter, you can get answers to important questions such as: Have you included XYZ Charity in your estate plans? Would you like more information about planned gifts to XYZ Charity?

Whether you write your own planned gifts newsletter or outsource the job, this tool has multiple benefits.

Why a Quarterly Newsletter Makes Sense

Whether you produce it on your own or outsource the job through a planned gifts consultant, distributing a quarterly planned gifts newsletter makes good sense. Here's why:

- **It helps to position your organization in the minds of would-be donors.** There are plenty of nonprofit organizations vying for planned gifts. The absence of ongoing planned gift messages will result in missed opportunities.

- **It allows you to educate would-be and existing donors.** A periodic newsletter enables you to provide constituents with technical information about various types of planned gifts and the benefits of each.

- **It supplements your efforts to build relationships.** Personal visits, phone calls, events and more all help to nurture relationships that will either result in planned gifts or help to solidify existing gifts.

- **It can be used to inspire others and recognize donors' generosity.** A planned gifts newsletter enables you to recognize planned gift donors and underscore the impact of gifts that have been realized.

Offer Sample Bequest Wording

To realize more charitable bequests, it's important that your organization show constituents just how easy it is to make a bequest.

Offer sample bequest wording from time to time in planned gift literature, in your regularly published newsletter or magazine, on your website and in other appropriate communications. Also, be sure to point out the benefits to the donor of leaving a bequest to your organization.

To the right is an example of bequest wording.

> **Remember (Name of Your Organization) In Your Estate Plans**
>
> I, (full name)) give, devise and bequeath to (Name of Your Charity), a (State) charitable corporation located in (City, State), the sum of $_____$ (or: _____ percent of the residue of my estate and or other personal property appropriately described) to be used for _____ (or: to be used as its Board of Trustees shall deem advisable to best promote (Name of Your Organization's) objectives).

PLANNED GIFTS NEWSLETTER & OTHER PRINTED COMMUNICATIONS

Justification for Producing Planned Gifts Newsletter In-house

It's common these days to outsource your planned gifts newsletter to a company that will slap your nonprofit's name and logo onto its canned publication. And although this process is clearly an option, it may not be the best option for organizations seeking to connect with donors and potential donors.

Producing your own planned gifts newsletter, while it may require additional staff time, has some distinct advantages over canned products. For example:

- Canned newsletters tend to be more technical in nature and diminish the human element. If they do include firsthand feature stories, chances are the person(s) being featured have no direct connection to your community. Producing your own newsletter allows you to include examples of real people within your circle of influence who are making or have made planned gifts to your nonprofit. These articles serve to inspire others to give while furthering relationships with subjects.

- Writing your own planned gifts newsletter allows you to focus on topics that you deem most appropriate at the time. Perhaps writing about some aspect of bequests will be of greater value than a canned article about lead trusts.

- Your own newsletter allows you to spoon-feed prospects with key information about your nonprofit and those you serve. Including topics that go beyond planned gifts helps build readerships and cultivates further interest in your mission and services.

- A more personalized newsletter will nurture your relationship with would-be donors. It's more like a letter from a friend.

In addition to these key points, you may find your in-house newsletter to be more cost effective than an outsourced product.

A Planned Gift Expectancies Idea

There are those who have indicated they have included your charity in their estate plans but have never made a significant outright gift. And there are those who have done both. To encourage the first group to consider making an outright gift (in addition to a planned gift), convince those who have done both to provide testimonials about why they are gratified they have made both kinds of gifts.

Bring Your Planned Gifts Newsletter to Life

Spotlighting feature stories about true-to-life gifts in every issue of your planned giving newsletter is worth the effort. Real life examples increase readership, make your newsletter more entertaining and readable, and illustrate in no uncertain terms what planned gifts can accomplish. Need ideas? Write about:

- How a gift came about.
- The people who made the gift.
- Why they made the type of planned gift they did.
- How the gift is making or will make a difference for your organization and those you serve.
- How the planned gift benefited the donor(s).
- People who have benefited from the planned gift.

Real-life examples help would-be donors to better visualize what they might accomplish with a planned gift.

Planned Gift Basics

How often do you invite the persons who make up your entire mailing list to consider your charity in estate plans? Be conscious about conveying that message regularly — in your newsletter or magazine, in presentations and during one-on-one calls.

PLANNED GIFTS NEWSLETTER & OTHER PRINTED COMMUNICATIONS

Seek Testimonials From Heirs of Planned Gift Donors

Here's a story idea for your upcoming planned gifts newsletter, constituency-wide newsletter or magazine:

Find children of planned gift donors who are more than willing to make positive comments about their parents' planned gift to your organization. Then build an article around their story.

What a positive message it would be for the son or daughter of a donor to say, in effect: "I'm so glad my parents are doing more than leaving their entire estate to me. They've taught me some valuable lessons about life, and this is just another great example of what it means to be a responsible and caring human being. I intend to follow their example and make charitable provisions in my estate as well."

Human interest topics such as this will be more likely to get read by others, and what a positive message to share with other planned gift prospects. Although it's necessary to communicate more technical information with planned gift prospects on your mailing list (e.g., tax benefits of particular planned gifts, descriptions of various planned gift vehicles), make a point to focus on the human element as well.

Don't hesitate to cultivate relationships with the children of planned gift donors.

Work to Identify, Confirm Planned Gift Expectancies

No matter how thorough your communications efforts, you may be unaware of individuals who have, on their own, made planned gift provisions that will one day benefit your organization.

Although some individuals choose not to share their charitable estate plans with you, being aware of such expectancies is undoubtedly helpful. Knowing a donor's wishes during his/her lifetime ensures that a planned gift will meet the desires of the donor as well as the needs of the recipient organization.

Take steps to encourage those among your constituency to inform you if they have made planned gift provisions. Publish a list of reasons for planned gift donors to confirm their plans with you.

Here is an example of such a list that you can edit to your organization's needs.

Please confirm your planned gift intentions with our office so that you...

1. Can receive the recognition and thanks you deserve.
2. Will be included in our Heritage Society and recognized.
3. Meet our staff and be assured your wishes will be fully honored.
4. Utilize staff expertise to choose the planned gift method that best meets your needs.
5. Verify that our organization is able to accept any special terms that may have been included in your gift.
6. May be informed of all tax advantages available based on your planned gift.
7. Make new friendships based on mutual goals shared with our charity.

One Simple Line Can Bring Big Results

Keeping planned giving in the minds of donors is an essential part of the solicitation process.

One way to do so is to add a line to every piece of printed material that leaves the office, including newsletters, brochures and stationery. Always add the sentence: "Have you included (name of your organization) in your will or living trust?"

Such a statement will serve as a constant reminder to make your charity their beneficiary.

PLANNED GIFTS NEWSLETTER & OTHER PRINTED COMMUNICATIONS

Planning Guidebooks Add Value to Donor Magazine

One proven way to engage major donors is to provide them with tools to achieve other desired goals while also supporting a worthy cause.

At Northwestern University Feinberg School of Medicine (Chicago, IL), development staff have produced a family-focused estate planning guidebook exploring ethical wills and methods for equitably distributing estate among children.

"Declining economic conditions shifted a lot of people's priorities away from charity and towards taking care of family first," says Joanna Riester, associate director of donor relations. "This booklet was chosen to show how people can take care of their loved ones and still further their ideals through charitable giving."

The guidebook is part of an ongoing series designed to augment the office's biannual donor magazine. Developed in collaboration with a third-party vendor, each booklet/magazine pairing shares a common theme and highlights a central topic such as a featured giving vehicle or timely piece of news.

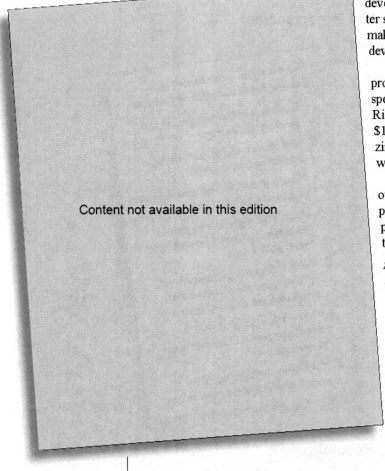

Content not available in this edition

While the booklets are distributed primarily to subscribers requesting further information, development staff use the booklets as well, Riester says, noting that the range of topics covered makes them a useful grab-and-go resource for development officers.

Much of the copy featured in guidebooks is provided by the vendor but can be tailored to specific donor stories or university events, says Riester. And while the materials cost $5,000 to $10,000 per issue (both guidebooks and magazine), Riester says she believes this is money well spent.

"Our donors are extremely generous, and we owe it to them to provide quality advice and planning options," she says. "These materials provide enough interest and substance to keep them turning the page and taking our next call."

Source: Joanna Riester, Associate Director of Donor Relations, Northwestern University Feinberg School of Medicine Office of Development, Chicago, IL. Phone (312) 503-8933. E-mail: J-riester@northwestern.edu

Development staff at Northwestern University's Feinberg School of Medicine (Chicago, IL) share this 14-page estate planning guidebook with major donors. See the book in its entirety at: http://www.feinberg.northwestern.edu/giving/pdfs/ FamilyFocused2010.pdf

How to Get a Planned Gifts Program Up and Running

STRATEGIES FOR MARKETING PLANNED GIFTS

What can you do to get the attention of more would-be donors? Besides some of the more obvious ideas outlined in other chapters — involving volunteers, estate planning seminars, newsletters — this chapter shares several ideas you may want to test and build upon.

How to Develop a Planned Giving Marketing Plan

Before you launch your next marketing effort, make sure to include the four processes critical to the success of any marketing effort, says Ann McPherson, a marketing consultant with PG Calc (Cambridge, MA).

Specifically, McPherson says, your marketing effort plan should: 1) establish and articulate objectives; 2) define the strategy; 3) execute the tactics of the program within the budget; and 4) measure, report and refine.

"These four processes should be applied to both your annual plans and individual marketing initiatives," McPherson says. "They operate sequentially and are dependent on one another."

Here, McPherson further defines the four critical elements:

1. **Establish and articulate objectives.** Select both tangible, measurable goals that you can realistically achieve, and less quantifiable goals, she says: "Well-defined objectives allow marketers to articulate clearly and succinctly what the marketing program seeks to achieve; making the objectives measurable allows them to demonstrate success when it happens — or learn valuable lessons if the result is less successful than forecasted. Regardless of your specific objectives, one of the most important activities you'll need to engage in if your program is going to succeed is a consideration of organizational support, both external and internal. By establishing enthusiasm for your efforts, you'll ensure you have continued support to see it through to your projected outcomes."

2. **Define the strategy.** Conducting a SWOT analysis (Strengths, Weaknesses, Opportunities, Threats) of your organization's mission will help you draft a precise, carefully crafted value proposition, position your organization relative to its competitors and peers, and develop a deep understanding of the target audiences to use as leverage in the marketing process, she says: "Your target audiences may be varied and each segment requires different messaging, as well as different frequency of communications and information. Target audiences for most planned giving officers include long-term annual fund donors and major gift donors, as they have indicated a certain charity as being of particular interest to them; communities of advisors, as they have proven to be influential when it comes to their clients' charitable intent; and existing planned gift donors, who are often likely to make a repeat gift arrangement."

3. **Execute the tactics of the program within the budget.** If a program's objectives have been well-defined and the strategic planning diligently conducted, the executive phase should proceed smoothly, she says. One way to help you execute the tactics of the program within the budget is to build a spreadsheet listing the various activities that will help you accomplish your objectives and the dates associated with their development and implementation, says McPherson. "A spreadsheet can help you manage each task and provide all of your team members with a visual summary of their responsibilities. Typical data captured include: 1) elapsed time for tasks, 2) the number of hours associated with each task, 3) the cost associated with each deliverable, and 4) ownership for each task. The process of building the spreadsheet is valuable in itself, since it requires a marketer to spell out every step required in the execution of the program and indicates dependencies."

4. **Measure, Report, Refine.** Because of lengthy cultivation cycles, assigning dollars raised to any particular campaign may be impossible, she says "Recognize, instead, that each campaign you pursue produces some success even if it's hard to measure. This does not mean that you should stop measuring. Rather, it is better to keep paying attention to best practices; reviewing, documenting and improving upon internal benchmarks; and most importantly, talking to donors and prospects about their thoughts."

Don't leave planned giving up to chance. Effective marketing can double and even triple the revenue generated by planned giving.

*Source: Ann McPherson, Marketing Consultant, PG Calc, Cambridge, MA.
Phone (888) 497-4970. E-mail: amcpherson@pgcalc.com. Website: www.pgcalc.com*

STRATEGIES FOR MARKETING PLANNED GIFTS

Consider Including a Planned Gift Option in Proposals

When preparing a written proposal for an individual, give thought to including a planned gift provision in addition to the outright gift you are seeking. Why? You have absolutely nothing to lose and much to gain.

Including a planned gift component helps the would-be donor think long-term about the gift he/she is about to make. It lets the donor know that once a pledge is made, that's not necessarily the end. It's a way of showing there's even more the donor could do to have a far greater impact.

Sample language that invites the donor to consider a planned gift in addition to the proposed outright gift:

Suggested Outright Gift: $250,000

Planned Gift Consideration

In addition to your outright gift, we invite you to consider a suitable planned gift as a way to add to this fund after your lifetime (or that of your spouse). There are a variety of planned gift vehicles that could be used to accomplish this goal. We welcome the opportunity to review these options in detail.

Approach Annual $1,000-plus Donors for Planned Gifts

How many annual contributors do you have at the $1,000-and-above level? What percentage of that group has made planned gift provisions for your organization?

Take steps to encourage and reassure those faithful and generous donors that their annual support will continue long after their lifetimes. Approach donors individually with invitations to make a planned gift that — after their lifetimes — will go to establish named endowment funds. Yearly interest from each fund will provide needed annual operations support (just as their annual contributions had done during their lifetimes).

Example: Assuming a donor had contributed $1,500 each year to your annual fund, it would take an endowment gift of $30,000 or more — based on an estimated 5 percent return — to yield what had been given yearly. In this instance, encourage the donor to consider a planned gift of not less than $30,000 to make certain his/her level of past support continues well into the future.

Make Your Presence Known Among Senior Citizens

Make yourself known in senior citizens' circles. Go where they go. Become familiar to them.

If a large part of your responsibility involves marketing planned gift opportunities, then it makes sense to gain greater visibility among senior citizens.

Whether you serve on boards of other organizations or attend public functions, consider those circumstances that position you in senior citizens' circles. For instance, serving as president of a group comprised of many retired individuals places you in a position of respect in the eyes of those with whom you associate.

Here are some additional examples:

❑ Retirement communities and residential settings.

❑ Clubs and civic groups: Kiwanis, Rotary, etc.

❑ Local coffee shops and senior citizen centers.

❑ Churches and synagogues.

❑ Particular social events: travelogue presentations, the golf course, bingo gatherings, etc.

STRATEGIES FOR MARKETING PLANNED GIFTS

Toolkit Helps to Promote Planned Gifts

The University of Washington's (Seattle, WA) office of development and alumni relations provides its staff with a planned giving options toolkit (www.devar.washington.edu/Toolkits/PlannedGiving/marketing.asp) that includes a planned giving options brochure; planned giving subtopic brochures (e.g., gifts in a will or trust, gifts of life insurance, etc.); print advertisements; and examples of specific planned giving direct mail pieces.

Here are eight more ways to promote planned gifts:

1. Develop a planned giving newsletter.
2. Include articles on planned giving in your internal and external newsletters.
3. Develop relationships with financial advisors.
4. Hold estate planning workshops and seminars.
5. Conduct group presentations to community groups in your target audience.
6. Create a planned giving educational video or purchase a canned video.
7. Send a direct mail piece to your donors announcing new legislation affecting planned giving. Include a buckslip that asks them if they would like to continue to receive news and information regarding planned gifts.
8. Create a planned giving buckslip and include it in thank-you notes and gift receipts.

Share the Story: 'Life of a Planned Gift'

Looking for more effective and creative ways to market planned gifts? Why not share a pictorial journal of someone who made a planned gift or is in the process of making a planned gift?

Whether you produce a DVD or video that can be distributed, create a podcast on your website, do a two-page spread in your magazine or a combination of all of these, the goal is to visually profile one individual's planned gift from beginning to end.

Here are two ways it might work:

1. Consider those who have made planned gifts in the past or a deceased individual whose bequest made a significant impact on your organization. Is there someone for whom you have photos and past correspondence available? Could you use your records to create a time line and summarize events leading up to that planned gift? Perhaps you can provide background on the donor, a description of the type of planned gift the donor established, when the planned gift became a reality, photos of those who benefited from the gift or how it impacted your organization.

2. If your files don't include an interesting past example, approach a living donor and begin to document that person and his/her gift for use at a future date. This approach could yield a great illustration for the future.

Ever considered documenting the progression and eventual impact of a planned gift? Now there's a testimonial!

Terminology Explains Contingent Bequest

Contingent bequest — Transfers property only when those named as primary beneficiaries predecease the testator or if the named beneficiaries refuse the bequest provision.

Sample Contingent Bequest Language

"In the event that (name of the primary beneficiary) does not survive me, I designate (legal name of charity) as the devisee of this bequest of (specify the amount in dollars or as a percentage of the estate or describe the noncash property that is the subject of the bequest)."

STRATEGIES FOR MARKETING PLANNED GIFTS

Approach Named Endowment Donors for Planned Gifts

Here's a way to encourage endowment donors to consider a planned gift.

If your organization already has a good number of named endowment gifts in place, make sure you're using a variety of methods that encourage those endowment donors to add to their funds with planned gifts. These donors make great planned gift prospects since they have already demonstrated their ability to make sizeable outright gifts to your organization. Plus, the addition of planned gifts will one day help to ensure that their endowments live up to their intended use far into the future.

Here are some ways to market planned gifts to endowment gift donors:

1. Get to know and meet regularly with all endowment gift donors.

2. Do an article about an endowment gift donor who added to his/her endowment with a planned gift.

3. Host an estate planning seminar geared specifically to endowment donors. Earmark a portion of the event to focus on issues related to your organization's endowment (e.g., policies, performance, investment philosophy, etc.).

4. When publishing lists of endowment donors, highlight those who will be adding to their funds with planned gifts.

5. When preparing annual updates for those who have established endowment funds, include what-if examples relating to possible planned gifts.

Practical Strategies for Promoting Bequests

Since bequests are the most popular form of planned giving, it makes sense to promote them on a continual basis to your constituency. Here are three varied strategies for keeping the topic of bequests before the public:

1. **During any type of public gathering, never miss an opportunity to invite those present to consider your charity in their estate plans.** Whether your invitation is accomplished in a subtle or direct manner, making mention of the topic says it's important to your organization's future. If appropriate, you can also stress that "if you have made provisions but have not informed us, please do."

2. **Don't be shy about publicizing the realization of a bequest.** The more examples seen by the public, the more they realize your organization must be worthy of such gifts, since so many persons have chosen your charity. These examples also provide you with additional opportunities to broadcast key messages: "Our board of trustees has approved a policy whereby all undesignated bequests will be directed to our endowment, thus perpetuating the donor's generosity for generations to come."

3. **Identify persons who have shared their intentions to include your charity in their estate plans and are willing to assist in encouraging others to do the same.** Determine the ways in which such persons would be willing to help you promote bequests — testimonials at public functions, profiles in your newsletter or magazine, accompanying you on planned gift visits — and make use of their example. Engaging such willing individuals in your planned gift program will make them feel even more committed to your cause.

Push Charitable Bequests

Based on research conducted by the National Committee on Planned Giving (Indianapolis, IN):

✓ 42 percent of Americans have wills.
✓ 8 percent say they have included charitable provisions in their wills.
✓ 14 percent say they have considered charitable provisions without being asked.
✓ 73 percent of donors leaving charitable bequests do not inform charities of their provisions.

Bottom line: Bequests are among the lowest cost, highest return gifts a charity can generate. Is your development shop putting in all the time and resources that your planned gifts program deserves?

STRATEGIES FOR MARKETING PLANNED GIFTS

Smaller Planned Gifts Are OK, Too

So often when we think of planned gifts, we think of six-figure bequests or more. But wouldn't you welcome a steady stream of $20,000 or even $5,000 gifts each year?

Keep your sights on large planned gifts, but encourage planned gifts of any size, recognizing that a steady stream of smaller planned gifts can be just as helpful as the occasional large bequest.

Many constituents don't consider a charitable planned gift, because they think a smaller one won't be needed or appreciated. So they dismiss the idea and decide to limit their gifts to those while they are living.

To encourage people to consider a planned gift, regardless of size, take these steps:

❑ Include articles in your planned gifts newsletter that talk about how even smaller bequests can positively impact your organization and those you serve. Be specific.

❑ Give equal publicity to realized smaller planned gifts as you do larger ones.

❑ When meeting one-on-one with would-be donors, emphasize the importance of all planned gifts regardless of their size.

❑ Encourage life insurance and similar gifts that don't require large outlays of money but will one day provide a sizeable gift after their lifetimes.

Don't let a focus on average gift size blind you to the impact reliable amounts of smaller gifts can have.

All Development Staff Should Help Promote Planned Gifts

The responsibility of planned gifts should not rest with one individual alone.

Each member of the advancement team — in fact, every employee within an organization — can and should assist with this ongoing effort.

Here's a sampling of ways you can encourage persons within your organization to assist with planned giving:

✓ Identify persons within your own circle of friends, relatives and contacts who may be planned gift prospects, and share their names with your planned gifts officer.

✓ Educate yourself. Meet with the planned gifts officer to learn how you would go about making a personal planned gift to learn more about how that would proceed.

✓ Include planned gifts prospects among your calls (after gaining approval from the planned gifts officer).

How to Get a Planned Gifts Program Up and Running, Second Edition.
Edited by Scott C. Stevenson.
© 2011 Stevenson, Inc. Published 2011 by Stevenson, Inc.

IDENTIFY, NURTURE AGENTS OF WEALTH

Agents of wealth — attorneys, trust officers, CPAs, financial planners and others who assist people in money matters — deserve your attention. Your ability to make them more aware of your nonprofit's planned gift worthiness and involve them in the life of your nonprofit, will influence your ultimate success. This chapter focuses on ways in which you can identify and nurture relationships with agents of wealth.

Build a Corps of Attorney Ambassadors

Anyone with experience in planned giving will tell you it's helpful to have attorneys out there batting on behalf of your organization.

But how does that come about? After all, attorneys will generally tell you that ethics prevents them from encouraging clients to make estate plans for a particular nonprofit. And that's true. However, when clients are the ones bringing up the topic of charitable gifts — seeking their attorney's advice — it's definitely in your nonprofit's best interest to have those attorneys familiar with your organization and the many ways in which you will gladly accept gifts.

That means it's important to establish rapport and respectful relationships with persons in the legal profession. It takes months, even years, to build a corps of attorneys who are sold on the value of your organization to the community, region and society.

Here are a few ways to begin building your corps of attorney ambassadors:

Develop a plan for cultivating meaningful relationships with attorneys and other agents of wealth.

- Make a point to meet one-on-one with attorneys in your area. Briefly summarize your organization's planned gift program for them and leave your business card. Then, make a point to stop by at least once a year to update them on your organization and examples of planned gifts your nonprofit has realized.

- Put those attorneys on your mailing list to receive your organization's newsletter or magazine. If you publish a regular planned gifts newsletter, be sure they receive that as well.

- Be sure your planned gifts advisory committee includes some attorneys. If possible, have attorney representation on your board of trustees as well.

- Cultivate attorney relationships by including them in estate planning workshops for your constituency. If you coordinate workshops in other communities as well, recruit attorneys from those locations to assist with your effort.

- When you come across a charitable gift article that would be useful or of interest to your attorney ambassadors, send them a copy along with a personal note.

- Host a reception or luncheon for your agents of wealth. Have your organization's CEO and other board members present to thank them for their interest in your insititution. Cite examples of how bequests and other planned gifts are making a noticeable difference for those you serve.

- When your agency realizes planned gifts, don't overlook those attorneys who were involved in the distribution of assets. They will be much more amiable when future opportunities present themselves if they have had a previously pleasant relationship.

Building a corps of attorney ambassadors is a long-term investment. It requires building respect for both you and the institution you represent. With a system in place, you can set annual objectives that include adding and cultivating a minimum number of these professionals to your centers of influence list each year.

Don't Hesitate to Get Expert Advice

If you're not an expert at planned gifts, don't attempt to answer prospects' questions if you're unsure of the answers. Instead, take the time to get the right answers. After all, planned gifts should be the result of careful consideration on the part of the donor, and your goal should be to help the donor arrive at a decision that he/she will feel positive about months and even years later.

Should a technical question arise, respond genuinely: "That's a good question, but one I need to research in order to give you the best possible advice. Let me get back to you on that one."

Then do whatever it takes to provide a knowledgbable response: research, meet with an attorney or planned gift expert or get the right professional involved with the prospect. Your primary goal, even beyond securing a planned gift, should be to assist the prospect to arrive at the best possible decision for him/her.

IDENTIFY, NURTURE AGENTS OF WEALTH

A Surefire Way to Cultivate Agents of Wealth

Agents of wealth — attorneys, trust officers, accountants and more — can be great allies in your effort to promote planned gifts. But it's not always that easy winning over the loyalty of these unbiased professionals.

To cultivate relationships with agents of wealth, invite them to submit an article for your planned gifts newsletter. Allowing a guest writer to share some planned giving expertise allows him/her to become involved and get some free publicity in the process.

Suggest these and other topics for your agents of wealth to author:

- Life Insurance: The Affordable Major Gift
- Have You Considered Gifting Your IRAs?
- Why a Life-estate Gift Might Be Your Best Option
- Benefit Your Heirs and (Name of Charity) at the Same Time
- Advantages of Testamentary Life-income Gifts
- Increase Retirement Income With a Charitable Gift Annuity
- The Charitable Lead Trust: How It Works and Might Benefit You
- Don't Get Caught Without a Will
- Teach Your Heirs by Leaving a Charitable Bequest

Requesting articles written by agents of wealth — attorneys, trust officers, CPAs and more — is a great way to engage them and get their names in the public's eye.

Build a Network of Estate Planning Professionals

Ever wish you had greater access to major donors and those who advise them? Why not build a professional network of your own?

For more than a decade, Pepperdine University's Center for Estate and Gift Planning has done just that with its Pepperdine Estate Planning Network (PEPNET), a dues-paying organization dedicated to connecting and developing estate planning professionals.

"We have estate planners, attorneys, CPAs, CLUs, financial planners, trust officers, even a few appraisers," Stephanie Buckley, center director, says of its 100-plus members.

The network centers on quarterly meetings featuring a range of charitable planning presentations. Overseen by center officials, the meetings provide networking opportunities, plus the chance to earn continuing education credit toward members' professional designation requirements. Members also receive publications, case studies and access to the center's planning experts and resources.

Maintaining such a program is not without tangible benefits. Buckley says that a number of significant gifts have come through PEPNET advisors, but stresses that her staff is glad to assist with any member's proposal, not just those directly benefiting Pepperdine.

"We like to say that there is no competition among lighthouses," she says. "If a gift helps Pepperdine, great. But if it helps someone else, that's great, too."

Source: Stephanie C. Buckley, Director, Center for Estate and Gift Planning, Pepperdine University, Malibu, CA. Phone (310) 506-4893. E-mail stephanie.buckley@pepperdine.edu. Website: www. pepperdine.edu/estateandgift/pepnet/default.htm

Building your own network of professionals is a great way to lay the foundation for long-term planned giving success.

PUBLICIZE PLANNED GIFTS, BUILD AWARENESS

What are you doing to build public awareness of your planned gifts program? How are you making the public more aware of those planned gifts that are positively impacting your nonprofit and those you serve? This chapter offers some ideas on how you can build awareness and gain more exposure for your planned gifts program.

Publicize Bequests to Receive More of Them

Publicizing the generosity of those who have made bequests will encourage others to consider similar acts of magnanimity. To make known how others have remembered your charity with a bequest:

1. Purchase and place in a prominent spot in your facility a specially designed wall hanging bearing names of those who have remembered your charity in their wills.

2. Tie undesignated bequests to a particular capital improvement or endowed fund and name it in honor of the donor.

3. Make mention of realized bequests in your publications and derive as much publicity as possible through media outlets.

4. Host an open house or reception once a bequest has been used to make an improvement or, if used for endowment, is beginning to make an impact.

If the donor has family, extend gratitude to them and keep them informed of how the donor's generosity is being recognized, add them to your mailing list and take other steps to embrace them as members of your charity's family.

Partner With Other Charities To Publicize a Joint Bequest

Now and then an individual will leave multiple bequests that benefit several charities. If that happens to your charity, make the most of the occasion by holding a joint press conference with the recipient charities to gain as much coverage as possible.

Pull the CEOs from the recipient charities together, allowing each to make statements to the press and take questions. The representatives can talk about how their gifts will be used and emphasize the impact their respective bequests will have on their missions.

The collaborative effort will draw far more attention to the donor's act of generosity and give you far greater exposure.

Seek Donor Testimonials

Give major donors a voice to recognize them and encourage others to give as well.

When a donor documents a planned gift to the Roland Park Country School (RPCS), Baltimore, MD, school officials ask for a brief testimonial, says Ginny Wood Delauney, assistant director of development and director of gift planning.

"We like to hear the donors' own voices, so we try not to alter what they write," Delauney says. "I usually send them a couple of examples so that they have an idea of what I would like from them.

"It is nice to show a variety of donors as well as an array of deferred gift types," she adds. "Most donors seem pleased to be asked to write something and hope that their testimonial will encourage others to make a planned gift to the school."

In addition to posting the testimonials on the school's planned giving Web page, school officials spotlight them in magazines and planned giving materials. "We write more in-depth profiles on donors ... for a number of reasons," says Delauney. "It could be because someone has recently passed away, their gift has been realized, and we want to acknowledge and honor them. It might also be because we want to highlight the particular planned gift vehicle that the donor chooses, such as a charitable remainder trust or an irrevocable bequest."

Roland Park Country School (Baltimore, MD) features major donor testimonials on its website, including this from a 1998 alum:

"It was because of my experiences and education at RPCS that I became the person I am today.

"It is for this reason that I wanted to give the School as much as I could afford, so I made a deferred gift in the form of a life insurance policy.

"Charitable life insurance policies provide a tax deduction to the donor while supporting RPCS in a most affordable way.

"It makes me proud that I have taken the initiative to help guarantee greater opportunities for future students."

Source: Ginny Wood Delauney, Assistant Director of Development, Director of Gift Planning, Roland Park Country School, Baltimore, MD.
Phone (410)323-5500, ext. 3139. E-mail: delauneyg@rpcs.org.
Website: http://www.legacy.vg/rpcs/giving/5.html

PUBLICIZE PLANNED GIFTS, BUILD AWARENESS

Ways to Publicize Realized Gifts

How are you making the public more aware of the planned gifts your nonprofit has received?

Exploit every means available to tell the story of donors and the impact of their gifts on your nonprofit and those you serve.

Develop a checklist of ways to tell those stories that may include:

1. Press releases and news conferences.

2. Television and radio interviews that convey a gift's impact.

3. A display case that lists all planned gift donors.

4. Feature stories in your publications that include donor testimonials.

5. Posting stories, testimonials and donor lists on your website.

6. Public recognition of living planned gift donors at events.

Planned Gifts Triggers

■ Key life events can cause donors to think about planned giving. Events that can trigger the desire for estate planning include the birth of a child or grandchild, the death of a friend or relative or the retirement of the donor.

Seek Real Planned Gift Stories

How often do you see planned gift literature describing in technical terms a charitable gift annuity or a charitable remainder trust, followed by a brief fictitious example to explain how each planned gift works?

Instead of fiction, go for fact. Ask friends of your organization who've made such gifts if you may share their stories.

While some planned gift donors prefer anonymity, others will be willing to share the story of their gifts if it helps encourage others to give.

Share as many details as possible. Tell how the gift is to be used, gift size, tax breaks realized as a result of the gift, the return the donor is receiving for the remainder of his/her life (and the life of his/her spouse), and more.

Each of these are valid sales tools, if you have donors ready and willing to share their stories. So ask them. Their willingness to help may surprise you.

ONLINE STRATEGIES

More and more nonprofits are using their websites as a way to increase awareness of planned gift opportunities and even to recognize and steward planned gift donors. Discover how other organizations are using the Internet as a way to introduce, educate, cultivate and steward donors and would-be donors.

Chart Illustrates Differences in Planned Gifts

To help educate planned gift prospects, many charities make use of charts to compare components and benefits of various types of planned gifts. Comparisons of gift annuities, pooled income trusts and other types of gifts are made on factors such as:

An everything-in-one graphic like the one shown here can be a good way to help potential supporters orient themselves to a range of options.

- Fund assets (cash, securities, etc.)

- Fixed or variable payments

- Deferral of payments

- Payout basis (fixed payments, portion of income, etc.)

- Income beneficiaries (one or two persons, multiple, etc.)

- Term of years option

- Investment approach

- Minimum gift required

- Minimum age of beneficiaries

- Charitable income tax deduction

- Capital gains avoidance

- Taxation of income payments

Oberlin College online planned gift comparison chart:

Content not available in this edition

Planned Gift Comparison Charts

Here are examples of charities' online planned gift comparison charts:

University of Wisconsin Foundation — http://uwfoundation.plannedgifts.org/chart.html

Oberlin College (Oberlin, OH) — www.oberlin.edu/giving/gp_compare.html

Taylor University (Upland, IN) — http://taylor.giftplans.org/index.php?cID=102

Sierra Club (San Francisco, CA) — www.sierraclub.org/giftplanning/comparison-chart/default.aspx

Springfield Foundation (Springfield, OH) — http://springfieldfoundation.org/waystogive.html

ONLINE STRATEGIES

Examples of Great Planned Giving Websites

New York Philharmonic — Go to the website, www.nyphil.org, click on the "Support" tab, then the "Planned Gifts" link. Select the "Pooled Income" link in the far left column for information on pooled income funds that includes charts and graphs showing historical annual valuation and income distributions.

WOI Radio Group (www.futurefocus.net/news_info.htm) — This site profiles various WOI Radio Group planned giving donors. It also has a planned giving glossary and a link to news and information about planned giving.

Websites of Interest

www.estateplanninglinks.com — For consumers and estate planning professionals, this site lists hundreds of timesaving links to estate planning, elder law and related websites.

www.pgresources.com/regs. html — Easy-to-review, state-by-state regulations for charitable gift annuities.

Draw Inspiration From These Online Examples

Devote a Web Page to Your Planned Gifts Club

To increase people's awareness of planned gift opportunities and recognition, devote a portion of your website to your planned gifts society or club. Below are some examples of nonprofits doing that:

Baltimore Symphony Orchestra (www. baltimoresymphony.planyourgift.org/heritage.php) — The Baltimore Symphony Orchestra's Legato Circle lists the benefits for those who have made planned gift provisions.

Vassar College (Poughkeepsie, NY) — http://development. vassar.edu/giftplanning/vcs/ — The Vassar College Society provides a gallery of photos from its annual luncheon.

Wheaton College (Wheaton, IL) — http://giving.wheaton. edu/main.taf?p=4,7 — The site includes a response form inviting anyone who has made planned gift provisions but not informed the college to do so.

Illustrate Planned Gifts Anyone Can Afford

Tufts Medical Center (Boston, MA), has web space (www.tuftsmedicalcenter.org/Giving/GiftPlanningMain/ default) that illustrates ways anyone can afford a gift that "doesn't affect your current lifestyle or your family's security."

Abbott Northwestern Hospital Foundation (Minneapolis, MN) offers a quiz (www.plan.gs/Quiz. do?orgId=713&quiId=9) that asks visitors, "How does your will measure up?"

Be Sensitive to Website Visitors Needs

The University of Portland's (Portland, OR) website allows visitors to increase or decrease the size of text (www.plan.gs/ Home.do?orgId=5277) — a particularly thoughtful addition for senior citizens who may prefer larger text.

Consider Adding Planned Gift Terms to Your Website

Rochester College (Rochester Hills, MI) — (www. futurefocus.net/rc/glossary.htm)

How to Get a Planned Gifts Program Up and Running, Second Edition.
Edited by Scott C. Stevenson.
© 2011 Stevenson, Inc. Published 2011 by Stevenson, Inc.

RECOGNITION AND STEWARDSHIP MEASURES

The ways in which you recognize and steward planned gift donors not only strengthens your relationship with them and acknowledges their generosity, but also plants seeds in the minds of others who may explore planned gifts for the first time.

Acknowledge Donors In Unique Ways

Q. **What unique ways are you acknowledging your planned giving donors?**

Donor Recognition Idea

Looking for a creative way to share the impact of a major gift with the donor who made it all happen? LaShon Anthony, small business consultant with visuals4 (Chicago, IL), shares an out-of-this-world method: name a star after the donor.

This opportunity is available through the International Star Registry (Ingleside, IL). Learn more at http://starregistry.com.

Source: LaShon Anthony, Small Business Consultant, visuals4, Chicago, IL.
E-mail: info@visuals4u.com.
Website: http://visuals4u.com

"One of the member benefits for our Benedictine Legacy Society is a Saint John's Estate Planning Binder. This binder has an embossed cover showing our Abbey Church, a major architectural touch point. It has plastic sleeves for holding documents related to a donor's estate plans, such as trust documents, will, advisor's contact information, etc. Each section has a log for noting the latest information additions.

"Some donors use it as the basic storage for their papers and keep it in a secure location. Others put photocopies of documents in the sleeves with notes describing the location of the original documents. We very strongly recommend that originals be placed in safety deposit boxes or other secure locations.

"Many donors have expressed appreciation for the usefulness of the book in two ways: It reminds them of what documents are important and also provides a copy of the documents for heirs to use to identify originals."

— *Jim Dwyer, Director of Planned Giving, Saint John's University and Abbey (Collegeville, MN)*

Five Rules for Preserving Expectancies

It's a major accomplishment every time you learn of someone who has included your organization in his/her estate plans, since many donors choose not to share that information during their lifetimes. But once you're aware of an expectancy, what are you doing to maintain or even solidify the relationship?

These five precepts will help ensure the donor won't reverse his/her estate plans:

It's important to strengthen relationships with those who have made planned gift provisions.

1. **Get a good reading on what matters most to the individual.** Understanding donors' personalities and motivations for giving will help direct the level of attention and/or anonymity they receive. Some like the attention while others prefer anonymity.

2. **Practice good stewardship even if it's years before you might realize the gift.** A young person who makes a commitment to contribute a life insurance policy, for instance, deserves the same attention as a senior citizen who has made a bequest.

3. **Have programs in place that recognize those who choose to be recognized.** While not everyone desires attention, you can develop programs recognizing those who do appreciate recognition — a heritage society with accompanying benefits, listings in your annual report and on a plaque in a public location of your facility, etc. Such programs let the public know you're in the business of accepting planned gifts as well.

4. **Keep the communication regular but varied in the method of delivery.** In addition to "broad brush" cultivation efforts — a quarterly planned gifts newsletter, a general newsletter or magazine, invitations to events, etc. — provide individual communications such as face-to-face meetings, personal correspondence and lunch with your CEO that keep these important persons involved and in the know.

5. **Honor donors' confidentiality.** Planned gifts are a very personal matter. Print "in strictest confidence" on planned gift communications and stress your high level of confidentiality whenever discussing planned gift matters.

RECOGNITION AND STEWARDSHIP MEASURES

Maintain Connections With Bequest Donors' Families

 "Do you involve scholarship recipients of older endowments (those with no living or known donor contacts) in stewardship activities, such as writing thank-you notes to donors, and attending your annual scholarship luncheon? If so, how?"

"Oftentimes we will use the students who are attached to endowed funds that no longer have a living donor to help us with our stewardship of donors who have expressed an intent to establish a scholarship through a bequest. This way all scholarship students are able to be involved, and we can 'steward' our bequest donors even though they do not yet have a student attached to their scholarship."

— *Laura Yeager, Stewardship Manager, Culver Academies (Culver, IN)*

"We always invite the student recipients of memorial scholarships to our annual scholarship event, even if there is no living donor contact. We then ask either the associate dean or the program head from the students' area of studies to present the scholarship on behalf of the family. We also give each student a brief bio about the person memorialized."

— *Susan Walters, Awards Coordinator, BCIT Foundation (Burnaby, British Columbia, Canada)*

"If we receive acknowledgment letters for an endowment with no contact, we try to send them to members of our planned giving society who decided to establish a scholarship after they pass. Doing this is good stewardship. It means that the letters are not wasted, and it's a nice touch for those individuals who will not see their gift in action during their lifetime."

— *Robin Banker, Assistant Director of Donor Relations, North Carolina State University (Raleigh, NC)*

"We do not ask students receiving scholarships for which we have no living contact persons to write letters or participate in our scholarship luncheon (we don't have room for all the students whose donors might choose to attend). However, we do invite people who have arranged to fund a scholarship through a planned gift to attend the luncheon, and we try to seat them with students with whom they may have common interests. They will never see the recipients of their scholarships, but they really enjoy the chance to meet current students."

— *Marcia Casais, Assistant Director, Advancement Communications, Drew University (Madison, NJ)*

Continuing to honor departed donors will appeal to current prospects interested in building an ongoing legacy.

Follow Up on Unexpected Bequests

Isn't it wonderful to be surprised by a bequest that comes "out of the blue?" It's sometimes surprising, however, how little follow-up takes place when that occurs. Maybe it's because no one on the development staff feels any real ownership of the unexpected gift.

One Midwest university received a surprise bequest from a graduate. Whether or not it was a mistake, no one from the institution took any action to follow up. No gift acknowledgment was sent to the graduate's widow. Nothing. To this day, those college officials don't realize the widow died with no heirs and an estate that amounted to $4 million.

It pays to follow up with surprise bequests.

RECOGNITION AND STEWARDSHIP MEASURES

Arrange Family Get-togethers for Named Funds

Philanthropy can and should become a family tradition. Along with stewarding individuals who have established named funds, be sure to include their family members in your stewardship efforts.

Why not arrange a series of individual family get-togethers to cultivate relationships with family members who may in time choose to add to these funds? Whether you meet for lunch at a local cafe or dinner in the donor's home, use this time to educate and share the impact these funds have on your organization and those you serve.

Here's some of what you might address in a session with family members:

1. When was the fund established, where does the fund currently stand and how has it grown over time?

2. What is the purpose of the fund? What are its unique attributes?

3. What has the fund accomplished since its inception? How has it positively impacted your organization and those you serve?

4. What more could be accomplished if the fund doubled or quadrupled in size over time?

5. How might family members be formally recognized if they add to this fund or establish named funds of their own?

How successful you are at organizing these family get-togethers will depend on the willingness and enthusiasm of the original donors to support your efforts. To help make your case, explain to them how such get-togethers will help engender to future generations that same philanthropic philosophy they obviously believe is important.

Create Interactive Donor Wall

RCB Awards (Milwaukee, WI) has developed an interactive donor recognition option that combines a traditional static donor wall with a functional and engaging electronic multimedia presentation.

Multimedia and interactivity will be increasingly important as technology becomes ever more sophisticated and personal.

The wall's interactive video touch screens allow an organization to create a personalized project by incorporating videos depicting its mission and programs, as well as donor stories and other elements.

"A good donor wall should be more than a list of names; it should be a showcase of your most significant achievements, an acknowledgement of your most generous supporters and a powerful statement about your purpose and vision," says Curt Denevan, sales and marketing manager. "It should be the first step in soliciting campaign donors. The viewer of every donor wall is a prospective donor of your organization. Does your wall talk to them?"

Design options allow organizations to create a wall with one large touch screen and/or several smaller touch screens. Cost depends on size, type of material used, number and size of touch screens and other elements. View a sample interactive donor wall at: www.youtube.com/watch?v=MgUK1qgwa7c

Source: Curt Denevan, Sales & Marketing Manager, RCB Awards, Milwaukee, WI. Phone (414) 479-9100. E-mail: curtd@rcbawards.com. Website: www.rcbdonorrecognition.com

PLANNED GIFT FORMS, POLICY ISSUES AND SAMPLES

This chapter offers some examples of useful forms and addresses some of the policy issues common to planned gifts programs. It also lists useful resources for any planned gifts office.

Referral Form Helps Garner Planned Gift Prospects

In what ways do you seek out new planned gift prospects? Do you or have you ever considered using a referral form as one way of identifying such individuals?

While it might be inappropriate to utilize a referral form in a mass appeal format, it could certainly prove to be a helpful tool among your centers of influence — planned gift advisory committee, board members, existing planned gift donors and others — as a way to encourage them to assist in your identification effort.

Such referral forms could be distributed on a quarterly or yearly basis to key persons who may be helpful in identifying planned gift prospects.

Use of the referral form stresses the importance of identifying new planned gift prospects and also offers a viable way for others to become involved in your planned giving effort.

As you distribute the forms to select individuals, help them understand ideal characteristics of planned gift prospects for your organization. Offer them tips on where to look for such prospects as well. In fact, it may be helpful to give your centers of influence some of the characteristics and circumstances surrounding past planned gift donors to your organization as a way of illustrating the types of individuals who may be prime candidates.

Sample planned gift prospect referral form:

CONFIDENTIAL

WHITLEY
COMMUNITY SCHOOLS
FOUNDATION

Planned Gift Prospect Referral Form

Prospect's Name _____
Address _____
City _____ State _____ ZIP _____
Phone (_____) _____ Approximate Age _____
Occupation (or former occupation) _____
Spouse's Name _____
   ❑ Living   ❑ Deceased   If living, approximate age_____
Spouse's Occupation _____
Number of Children _____

Children's Names	Location	Occupation

Relationship (if any) to our organization _____

Why do you think this individual might make a good planned gift prospect for our organization?

Why might this individual be inclined to consider a planned gift to our organization?

Would you be willing to assist in introducing a staff person to this individual?

Would you be willing to assist in the cultivation of this individual?

This individual was referred by _____ Date of referral _____

PLANNED GIFT FORMS, POLICY ISSUES AND SAMPLES

Make Use of a Charitable Bequest Intent Form

What are you doing to encourage donors to make you aware of their planned gifts? Since it's not uncommon for as few as one-third of a charity's donors to have informed the charitable beneficiary of their bequest, it's important to encourage everyone that it's in their best interest to inform you of their provisions.

To help accomplish that, a charitable bequest intent form is a useful tool. You can share the form with planned gift prospects during one-on-one visits, make the forms available in your planned gifts newsletter, distribute them to key locations and also make the form available on your website.

Increase the percentage of planned gift donors who have informed you of their provisions by making use of this form.

Giving supporters a simple way to share their charitable bequest intentions will assist your planning and income projections.

Sample bequest intent form:

Content not available in this edition

PLANNED GIFT FORMS, POLICY ISSUES AND SAMPLES

Policy Should Address Surprise Bequests

If your nonprofit was to receive a surprise bequest for $200,000 — with no strings attached — what would you do with it?

Unfortunately, most budget-strapped nonprofits would spend it as fast as it came in to pay bills or start new programs with no future source of funding to support them.

If your organization receives "manna from heaven" in the form of a major gift, think twice before spending it. Have a gift acceptance policy that addresses this issue.

If you don't have one, establish an endowment fund in the donor's name and use only the interest from the principal to fund whatever you deem a priority.

Think about it: With a $200,000 gift you could spend $20,000 a year for 10 years, and it's gone, or you could invest the funds and spend the annual interest ($10,000 a year at five percent) for generations to come.

As strapped as you may be for resources, the choice should be a no-brainer.

What does your nonprofit do when it receives an unexpected, unrestricted bequest? Do you have a policy that addresses this?

Have a Policy for Accepting Life Insurance

Life insurance is often referred to as "the major gift that anyone can afford to give" because a person can make a very substantial planned gift at minimum cost. If you plan to encourage life insurance gifts, however, it's important that you have a board-approved policy in place for accepting such gifts.

A charity can encounter difficulties with life insurance gifts when:

- The charity is not named irrevocable owner of the policy;

- The policy includes beneficiaries in addition to the charity;

- The policy is not paid up in full; or

- The donor stops making annual gifts equal to the amount of unpaid premiums.

Sample Wording for Acceptance of Life Insurance Policies

(Name of Organization) may accept a life insurance policy as a gift if (Name of Organization) is named irrevocable owner and sole beneficiary. The gift is valued at its replacement cost for paid-up policies. The value of a non-paid-up policy is determined by adding to the interpolated terminal reserve plus any unearned premium and accrued dividends, less any policy loan. The cash surrender value and any premium paid by the donor should be recorded as gift revenue and as an asset on the balance sheet. Any premiums due are the responsibility of the donor. If the insurance policy lapses for nonpayment prior to maturity because a donor fails to provide for premium payments, (Name of Organization) may redeem the policy.

Acceptance Policy: Gifts of Life Insurance

A. (Name of Organization) will accept life insurance policies as gifts only when named as the irrevocable owner and beneficiary of 100 percent of the policy.

B. If the policy is paid up, the value of the gift for (Name of Organization)'s gift crediting and accounting purposes is the policy's replacement cost.

C. If the policy is partially paid up, the value of the gift will be considered the policy's cash surrender value.

PLANNED GIFT FORMS, POLICY ISSUES AND SAMPLES

Gift Acknowledgement Protocols Reduce Confusion, Lessen Mistakes

Scott Fendley, Principal, SF Consulting (Eden Prairie, MN), shares a detailed acknowledgement policy he developed for Wabash College (Crawfordsville, IN):

PROTOCOL FOR CAMPAIGN GIFT ACKNOWLEDGEMENT

The baseline or default response to gifts and/or pledges is:

All gifts to the College will be acknowledged by an official receipt thank you letter within two working days of the arrival of the gift on campus.

Annual donors of $250-999 will receive a letter from the Chair of the ... Foundation at the beginning of the month after the gift is received. ...

Donors of $1,000+ will receive a letter from the Chair of the 1832 Society at the beginning of the month after the gift is received. (Trustees will not receive this letter).Any changes in gift club status will be noted.

Phonathon pledges will be acknowledged in writing immediately after the pledge is made via handwritten note from student caller who took the pledge.

The Director of the Greater Wabash Foundation will acknowledge all pledges (excluding phonathon pledges) of $1-999. ... within 48 hours of receipt.

The Dean for Advancement will review all gifts and pledge payments of $1,000 and above and add personal acknowledgements, as appropriate, within 48 hours of receipt of the gift or pledge payment.

The Chairman of the Campaign will acknowledge outright gifts and pledges of $10,000 and above.

Documented bequests, trusts, life insurance gifts, and other planned giving vehicles that have been confirmed (not matured) shall be acknowledged by the Director of Major Gifts within 48 hours of notification for all gifts up to $100,000.The Dean for Advancement shall acknowledge any confirmed planned gift of $100,000 and above.The Dean for Advancement and the Director of Major and Planned Giving will advise the President of the College regarding the donors he should acknowledge.

The President of the College will be provided a list of all donors who have made a gift of $1,000 or more for his personal acknowledgements.

The Dean for Advancement will acknowledge all gifts and pledges from trustees and members of the board of the National Association of Wabash Men....

The Dean for Advancement and Chairman of the Faculty/Staff Campaign will acknowledge any pledge or gift made by a faculty or staff member. ...

The Dean for Advancement will acknowledge any gift from the Independent Colleges of Indiana.

The Senior Advancement Officer and Coordinator of Volunteer Services will acknowledge any gifts from non-alumni or non-parent owned corporations and all foundations, excluding matching gifts from corporations.

When a matching gift is received, a letter to the donor will be generated and signed by the Director of the Greater Wabash Foundation, excluding trustees. Matching gift companies will receive a receipt only.

Any alumni-owned or parent-owned business that makes a gift will be acknowledged as if the individual owner made the gift.

Letters acknowledging the receipt of memorial gifts, without specifying the gift amount, will be sent to the appropriate person in the family by the Dean for Advancement once a month.

When a gift of stock is made, the valuation ... will be included in the receipt thank you letter, which will be signed by the Dean for Advancement.

If volunteers give their expenses to the College as an in-kind gift instead of reimbursement, the Senior Advancement Officer and Coordinator of Volunteer Services will acknowledge the gift with a thank you letter.

Upon receipt of the final pledge payment (excluding phonathon pledges), a letter of acknowledgement from the Dean for Advancement will be generated thanking the donor for the completion of the pledge.

All letters will be changed quarterly, or as needed to refresh the content and reflect on recent news of the College.These letters will be prepared or reviewed by the Director of Campaign Communications.

(The policy also includes sections detailing special recognition of gifts, as well as how to issue pledge reminders.)

Acknowledging major gifts on the fly may cause important details to fall through the cracks, says Scott Fendley, principal, SF Consulting (Eden Prairie, MN).

That's why organizations should put gift acknowledgement policies in writing. Says Fendley, "Written acknowledgment policies prevent confusion, duplication of efforts, and 'I thought someone else did that,' kinds of situations."

Create policies that are as detailed as possible, he says. Specifically, gift acknowledgement forms should:

- Codify individual staff roles for as many common situations as possible.
- Describe in detail (mailings, signatures, time frames) responses to all gift sizes and program(s) supported.
- Clarify what donors will be invited to what events at what level for different gifts.

Granularity is also important in effective policies, Fendley says, enabling database software to be programmed to automate response actions while ensuring a continuity of response as development staff come and go.

Acknowledgement protocols are particularly useful with more esoteric planned giving vehicles such as memorial gifts, says Fendley, noting that heirs and survivors can be easily overlooked or forgotten.

Acknowledgement policies are best developed by advancement staff with input from senior leadership, says Fendley, and should include input from services and operations staff, as these departments are often involved with implementing, automating and executing policies.

Source: Scott Fendley, Principal, SF Consulting, Eden Prairie, MN. Phone (317) 445-0948. E-mail: scott@sfconsultingnow.com. Website: www.sfconsultingnow.com

PLANNED GIFT FORMS, POLICY ISSUES AND SAMPLES

Help Planned Gift Prospects Visualize What They Are Capable of Doing

It's been demonstrated time and again that most planned gifts are given based on personal gratification of some form. Certainly tax consequences play a role in the gift giving process, but are generally secondary to fulfilling one or more personal needs.

So if most planned gifts are driven by some form of personal gratification — to help others and society, to leave a lasting legacy, to honor or memorialize someone — a donor's ability to visualize what his/her gift will accomplish is key to its realization.

Your ability to illustrate the before and after of a planned gift will play a critical role in convincing the would-be donor to commit. Your preparation in painting a picture of what a planned gift will accomplish for your institution and those you serve will help the prospect begin to experience the personal need — helping others, making a difference, ego gratification — that will make the individual want to make a bequest or some other form of a planned gift.

That's why it's so important to visualize what could be as you meet with and cultivate planned gift prospects. It's not enough to know the technical aspects and tax consequences of various planned gifts.

Utilize these techniques to help the prospect visualize how his/her planned gift could make a noticeable difference:

- Provide personal tours of your facilities, pointing out present services and comparing them to what could be offered with the realization of a major gift.

- As you meet with prospects, share and leave with them printed illustrations of named gift opportunities. One illustration may, for instance, describe what a $50,000 gift could accomplish in providing annual scholarships for needy students. Another may help to visualize how an endowed landscaping and maintenance fund will enhance your organization's environment and maintain it for years to come.

- Share specific examples of what past donors' bequests are accomplishing for your organization. In fact, share examples of what other donors' planned gifts have accomplished for other institutions. This is simply another way of visualizing what could happen if sufficient funds are available.

In addition to helping donors see just what their gifts will accomplish, it's important to help them visualize the mechanics of how their gift is spent or invested (as in the case of an endowed gift). The more they understand, the more comfortable they will become in turning visions into reality.

Sample Personalized Illustration of a Naming Gift Opportunity:

Cosgrove University
Preparing Tomorrow's Leaders Today

NAMING GIFT CONSIDERATION

THE MARGARET AND TAYLOR ELLINGSON ENDOWED SCHOLARSHIP

Suggested Gift Amount: $100,000

Intent of Bequest
To assist junior and senior women attending Cosgrove University who intend to pursue health-related careers. Eligible students must have maintained a 3.4 grade point average or higher during their freshman and sophmore years. Financial need should also be taken into consideration.

How the Funds Will Be Invested
Once this $100,000 bequest is realized, it will be invested as a part of Cosgrove University's endowment portfolio. (See attached endowment report.) Annual interest from the fund will be awarded to deserving students who meet the guidelines set forth by Margaret and Taylor Ellingson. In recent years, the university's board of directors has approved an annual payout of 7 percent to ensure the preservation of the gift's principal for generations to come.

Therefore, if the annual interest rate remains constant, $7,000 will be available each year for scholarship awards.

Procedure for Annual Awards
At the request of Margaret and Taylor Ellingson, annual awards will be made through the Office of Financial Aid in cooperation with faculty representatives from the science/health-related disciplines.

Preparing Future Generations of Caring Health Professionals
Consider, for example, seven deserving Cosgrove University students each receiving a $1,000 award in any given year. Using that example, a gift such as this could potentially assist as many as 70 students throughout one decade receive a degree who might not otherwise be able to do so.

Over a 10-year period, as many as 70 graduates could be moving on to seek additional education or entering health-related careers. What a marvelous way to help so many young people! What a marvelous investment in our society's future!

How to Get a Planned Gifts Program Up and Running, Second Edition.
Edited by Scott C. Stevenson.
© 2011 Stevenson, Inc. Published 2011 by Stevenson, Inc.

APPENDIX

Resources for the Planned Gifts Professional

Following is a partial list of resources for the planned gifts professional:

Access International (www.accessint.com/drilldown.asp?pageID=47&mainparent=25) — Software provider.

American College of Trust and Estate Counsel (www.actec.org) — Nonprofit association of lawyers who advise clients in estate planning and other areas of expertise.

American Council on Gift Annuities (www.acga-web.org) — Provides educational and other services to American charities regarding gift annuities and other forms of planned gifts.

American Institute for Philanthropic Studies (www.plannedgivingedu.com) — Provides planned giving professionals and others with the knowledge and skills required to implement and maintain a successful gift planning program.

Blackbaud Analytics (www.blackbaud-analytics.com/planned-gifts.htm) — Software provider.

Canadian Association of Gift Planners (www.cagp-acpdp.org/en/default.aspx) — Supports philanthropy by fostering the development and growth of gift planning. The association creates awareness, provides education and is an advocate of charitable giving.

Crescendo Interactive (www.crescendointeractive.com) — Software, software design.

European Association of Gift Planning (www.eapg.org.uk) — Membership network which seeks to ensure the best possible practice in planned giving and cross-border philanthropy.

Financial Planning Association (www.fpanet.org) — Leadership and advocacy organization representing the financial planning community.

Gift and Estate Resources for Professionals (http://gift-estate.com) — A compendium of information for planned gift professionals.

John Brown Limited (www.johnbrownlimited.com) — Company provides strategy for planned giving and other programs.

Leave a Legacy (www.leavealegacy.org/index.asp) — LEAVE A LEGACY® is a nationwide effort designed to inspire people to make a charitable bequest.

National Association of Estate Planners and Councils (www.naepc.org) — Professional estate planners and affiliated estate planning councils focused on establishing and monitoring the highest professional and educational standards.

PG Calc (www.pgcalc.com/index.htm) — Company provides expertise in products and services for charitable gift planning and planned gift administration.

Pentera Inc. (www.pentera.com) — Planned gift assistance from newsletters to websites to brochures and more.

Planned Giving Design Center (www.pgdc.com) — A national network of hosting organizations that provide members with content on charitable taxation and planned giving.

Planned Giving Resources (www.pgresources.com) — The preeminent association for professionals in charitable gift planning field.

R&R Newkirk (www.rrnewkirk.com) — Providing planned gift promotional programs and training.

Sinclair, Townes & Company (www.sinclairtownes.com) — Provides comprehensive fundraising consulting services and planned gift publications.

Taxwise Giving & Philanthropy Tax Institute (www.taxwisegiving.com) — Conrad Teitell's advice and publications on charitable giving.

The Center on Philanthropy (www.philanthropy.iupui.edu) — Leading academic center dedicated to increasing the understanding of philanthropy and improving its practice through research, teaching, public service and public affairs.

The International Association of Advisors in Philanthropy (www.advisorsinphilanthropy.org) — A network of professional advisors who are devoted to mastering and promoting the principles and practices of client-centered planning.

The Stelter Company (www.stelter.com) — Assists charitable organizations by writing, designing, producing and distributing high-quality direct mail newsletters, collateral material and Internet-based products.

Lightning Source UK Ltd.
Milton Keynes UK
UKOW01f0823020813

214783UK00006B/172/P